THE MYSTIC'S GIFT

A story about loss, letting go...
and learning to soar

SKIP JOHNSON

"We must be willing to let go of the life we planned so as to have the life that is waiting for us."

—Joseph Campbell

Editing by Terry Stafford Wordsmithery
Cover Illustration and Interior Design by Dino Marino

ISBN Paperback: 978-1-7352511-3-4
ISBN eBook: 978-1-7352511-4-1

Other Books by Skip Johnson

See all books at www.skipjohnsonauthor.com

The Statue's Secret

Prominent Newport lawyer David Langley is a tormented man consumed by anxiety, guilt, and regret as his world falls apart more and more each day.

Until . . .

He fortuitously comes across an ancient Caribbean statue, which is soon verified as one of the most magnificent, sacred artifacts ever unearthed.

One with a unique blessing bestowed upon it for the benefit of its fourteenth century owner—and for all future owners . . .

A blessing that it seems could finally lead David on a path to a transformed life.

That is, *if* David can find his way to a mystical meeting with three wise, carefully chosen mentors at a remote location deep within the Dominican Republic jungle . . . within 48 hours.

Otherwise, the statue and its remarkable gift will vanish forever.

As David frantically, desperately makes his way to his final Dominican destination and the opportunity for an inspired new life, you'll find yourself enthusiastically cheering him on every step of the way.

Then, at some point you may realize the one who is truly on the journey . . . is *you*.

The Lottery Winner's Greatest Ride

When Phillip Westford won the biggest lottery in history, he never dreamed there would be a price to pay.

A very *large* price that would shake his world to the core . . .

But just when he is at his breaking point, Phillip meets a mysterious old Irishman named Patrick O'Rourke who claims he knows the secret for getting the distraught young man back to happiness.

That is, *if* Phillip is willing to undertake a trek to find three wise mentors across the globe.

Join Phillip on a magnificent train ride as he shares the inspiring, incredible story of his journey of transformation with Juliette McKelvey—a young journalist who is on her own desperate journey to rebuild her crumbling life.

It's a ride to happiness you'll soon realize . . . you were *destined* to be on.

The Treasure in Antigua

(Book 3 in The Mystic's Gift/Royce Holloway series)

Take a spellbinding journey with Royce Holloway as he crosses the magnificent island of Antigua in search of an elusive, sacred treasure which has the potential to change him forever . . . and change the world.

Along the way, Royce meets wise, inspirational mentors from all walks of life, who somehow seem part of a mysterious, bigger plan to guide him in reaching his destination.

Mentors who share unique stories of courage, belief, and determination in overcoming their personal pain and suffering— to eventually find their own treasures.

Join Royce on this captivating, spiritual Caribbean adventure as he learns eye-opening lessons that take him to a level of powerful, courageous, and compassionate living he never knew existed.

Lessons that can do the same for *you* . . .

The Gentleman's Journey:
A Heartwarming Story of Courage, Compassion, and Wisdom
(Book 2 in The Mystic's Gift/Royce Holloway series)

Five years after six transformative lessons from an ancient, sacred book were discreetly shared with Royce Holloway, he's now determined to use his gifts to positively impact the world at a whole new level. But while visiting the enchanting Georgia coast on a short sabbatical, he meets a mysterious world traveler whose mesmerizing words of wisdom put Royce on track toward a destiny he could never have imagined . . .

Hidden Jewels of Happiness:
*Powerful Essays for Finding and Savoring
the Gifts on Your Journey*

A book of wisdom, encouragement, and empowerment
for dealing with life's daily challenges. Let Skip show you
the seemingly hidden gifts that are all around us, waiting
to be found and enjoyed. You'll feel inspired, enlightened,
and happier as you read each and every page.

Grateful for Everything:
*Learning, Living, and Loving
the Great Game of Life*

A blueprint for using the power of gratitude to increase
your happiness and fulfillment. You'll find useful,
specific tools and ideas for turning your life into a great
game to play instead of a dreary battle to fight.

DEDICATION

To my courageous and compassionate daughters,
Betsy and Emily, who have been my supportive and
enthusiastic storytelling audience since they were
small children, I lovingly dedicate this book.

TABLE OF CONTENTS

MYSTIC

noun

/ˈmɪstɪk/

a person who uses prayer and meditation to try to become united with God or to understand important things that are beyond normal human understanding

—Oxford Learner's Dictionaries

CHAPTER 1

Royce Holloway was exhausted.

It had been three months since the accident, and he felt as if he hadn't slept in those ninety long days.

Thoughts raced through his head as he lay despondently in the empty bed, wondering when things would get better. After all, life had changed so quickly for him. Could it possibly change *back* at the same pace?

It occurred to him that type of thinking was pure nonsense. It would be a slow road getting back anywhere close to normal—if ever. The old saying, "Life is what happens to you when you are making other plans," popped into his head. Everything had been going so well. He had felt almost bulletproof—like his life was on track toward permanent success—a lucrative and fulfilling writing career, a happy marriage, two wonderful, healthy daughters, and a gorgeous home in the woods. Life was good.

Then, in a blink of an eye, he was a forty-two-year-old widower, a single father, and a broken man who wondered how he could possibly move on.

Royce rolled over and buried his head in the pillow to escape from the world. The pity-party ended quickly, however, as his phone rang loudly on the nightstand. His life-long friend, Stewart Edge, was calling. It was early, and he didn't feel like talking, but Royce picked up the phone anyway.

Stewart could barely contain his enthusiasm as he blurted out, "Royce, I've got someone you have to meet."

Royce gently but firmly reminded him of the time. "Buddy, it's seven in the morning. Couldn't you wait a while? Besides, I don't feel like talking to anyone."

Stewart chided him. "Look, lazy man. I'm telling you; you need to meet her. She's a master gardener, which I guess is cool enough, but she's not just *any* master gardener. I think she's some kind of philosopher or something." Royce's easily excitable friend chuckled a bit but then added, "Seriously, I've gotten to know her a little lately, and not only is she incredibly knowledgeable of her craft, she's one of the wisest people I think I've ever met. Plus," he quietly added, "you need to get out a little bit and meet some folks, pal. It's been months."

As much as he didn't want to admit it, Royce knew his buddy was right. The gardener did sound kind of interesting, so maybe it would at least be a diversion. The day before, he had dropped off his kids at camp for two weeks, which meant he would likely be sitting home in his large house by himself.

"She only lives about ten minutes away," Stewart said.

"Okay, might as well. Nothing ventured, nothing gained, as they say."

"Great, I'll set it up. But Royce, one really important tip. . ."

"What's that?" Royce asked.

"You're a writer. Don't use clichés like that."

The two laughed, and at the same time, for the first time since February 7th, Royce was suddenly aware of the beautiful early morning sun rising outside his window. *Time with the gardener might be good for me after all,* he thought.

Stewart arranged the meeting between Royce and the "gardening Zen master" for the following day. That morning, for the first time since everything happened, Royce felt a bit of pleasure in getting out of bed and going somewhere of potential interest.

He tried to keep his expectations realistic, but Royce couldn't help feeling eager and curious. His short drive to her home was filled with daydreams, memories, and unanswerable questions spoken out loud to himself—or maybe to God. He wasn't sure—but lately it was something he found himself doing quite often.

Once he arrived and parked his car, there was a short path through the woods that led to the gardener's cottage in the Georgia countryside. He was immediately taken aback as he came to the end of a thicket of pines, and the house came into view. He found himself surrounded by some of the most beautiful gardens he had ever seen—pockets of flowers, plants, and stunning rock formations. He felt as if he had entered the garden of the gods. He was amazed by the magnificent colors, variety, and symmetry she'd incorporated into her work.

Royce thought about his own gardening skills—or lack of—and had to chuckle. He could write a full-length book with ease, but when it came to gardening, he seemed to be only adept at growing nice, healthy weeds. It made everything else he saw even more impressive.

As he approached the front door, the owner stepped out, extended her hand, and greeted him like an old friend. "Hi, you must be Royce," she said, smiling. "I'm Maya. It's so good to meet you. Can I get you some tea or coffee?"

She had a slight accent, which added to the beauty of her voice. It was a dialect he had heard before from one of his many travels—maybe to the Far East. "No, thank you, ma'am," he replied with his soft Southern drawl. "I just had my fill of coffee on the way here.

Besides, I can already tell I am going to have a lot of questions for you out here in your gardens." He grinned.

She threw her head back and laughed easily. "Well, I'll do my best to answer them one by one. But I'll warn you; I'm a little slow getting started in the mornings. And one more thing," she added. "I haven't lived in the South that long, but I can't seem to get used to being called 'ma'am.' You'll simply *have* to call me Maya."

Royce felt himself blushing. "Will do, Maya. Sorry, old habits die hard, I guess. Just the way I was raised."

Something about this gentle woman resonated with Royce. She certainly was attractive, but there was *something* else. She had a compassionate, carefree manner and her long, flowing dark hair gave her an almost spiritual presence. Royce guessed she was in her early sixties, but because her light brown skin appeared soft and wrinkle-free, she could have easily passed for twenty years younger.

They walked over to one of her spectacular rock gardens, and Royce began his quest for knowledge about this woman and her skills. "Okay," he said, "here we go. My friend told me you could make a beautiful garden in the most difficult conditions. Is that true?"

She smiled and quickly replied, "Well, you know difficulty is really a state of mind, isn't it?" Before he could respond, she added, "I think that our difficulties more often arise not from the work before us, but from our relationship with that work. It's purely perspective."

Hmm . . . that's not the answer I expected, Royce thought. His line of questioning continued. "What's your favorite project—the favorite garden that you have created? A flower garden, a rock garden, maybe a vegetable garden you created somewhere?"

Her response was swift and sure. "My favorite garden is the one I'm working on right now," she said with a smile.

"I would love to see it," he said excitedly.

"Well, what I actually meant was that my favorite garden is whichever one I am working on at the time. Right now, it is the one in front of you. Last week, my favorite was the garden with the sunflowers you passed as you walked up to my home. I finished it last Thursday."

"Oh, I see. Similar to how parents try not to show partiality to any of their children, huh?"

"Something like that," she said. "I pour my heart into every project, so as I'm working, a high level of engagement just seems to lead me to loving every garden equally—but often in different ways."

Royce wondered aloud, "Have any of them ever *not* turned out well?"

She smiled and then shook her head. "I don't think like that. I mean, I hope people love what I do, but I don't get swayed by the opinions of the crowd either way. When I use my gifts to the best of my ability, I really can't look at any project as unsuccessful."

Yep, this is no ordinary gardener, he thought.

As if reading his mind, she smiled and said, "Gardening is a lot like life, isn't it, Royce?"

"You took the words right out of my mouth," he said with a big grin.

"It can be described as a kind of *amor fati,*" Maya said.

At that point, Royce was *really* impressed. As he'd been a political science major in college, he realized she was quoting the philosopher Frederick Nietzsche. "Amor fati—the love of fate," he chimed in.

"Bravo," she replied happily. "I see my gardening and my life like this; the conditions are always ideal. Wherever I am, and whatever garden I'm working on, that's the hand I have been dealt—it's simply part of my journey, and it's where I am supposed to be at that time. I will use that place, whether it's a literal or a figurative place, to learn from and to allow me to grow. Whatever the environment and whatever happens, I will use the conditions to make me a stronger, wiser, more compassionate person and to contribute to the greater good by leaving things more beautiful when I go."

Royce wasn't sure how this woman connected with him so quickly, but it already seemed as if they had known each other for a lifetime—as if she understood his thoughts. Maya smiled softly and added, "Royce, as a young woman, I realized after many years of constantly searching for perfect locations, I was wasting a lot of time, effort, and opportunities to use my skills to beautify things—all because the places I had found didn't seem just right. Now, I have a different perspective. I've made the decision that 'just right' is pretty much wherever I find myself."

"You know, gardening really *is* like life. I think I understand that now," Royce admitted.

Her smile seemed to light up the entire garden. "Yes, my friend," she agreed.

Royce felt so many emotions, but he continued his questioning. "How long does it take to put together these masterpieces?"

"As long as each one needs—not more, not less," she quickly replied.

"Of course," he said with an understanding smile. Odd as it seemed, he again felt he was starting to know this fascinating woman on a strangely deep level after only a few hours.

She continued, "Royce, it's time for me to get back to my work, but let me leave you with this thought; regardless of the conditions each of us face, I believe we can figure out a way to add beauty and make things better, so we won't waste an experience or a place. Now don't get me wrong, it's not always easy or what some would call perfect. Some places tend to have lots of weeds and lots of poor dirt, and there are places which would seem just plain awful to many folks. But if we look beyond that and see that these are just the conditions or circumstances that we've been given, we can simply get to work, trust the outcome, and intuitively know that we are being led in the right direction. When we have this attitude, we won't be disappointed with the results. Who knows, we may even change the world."

Change the world? As strange as most people might think that statement was, Royce somehow believed her. He had the feeling that maybe this woman *already* had somehow changed the world . . . and was continuing to do so.

Maya reached out her hand and gently clasped his as she said goodbye. When she did, he felt that unexplainable connection again. "I would love for you to come back if you'd like," she said. "It was truly a pleasure to spend time with you."

Surprising even himself, and without hesitation, Royce blurted out, "What about tomorrow?"

Maya smiled, responding as if she had already anticipated the answer. "That would be fine, Royce. In fact, I think we have more to talk about than you might realize."

CHAPTER 2

When he arrived home late that afternoon, Royce reflected on the irony. As a self-help author, he wrote about seizing every day with excitement and positive anticipation. Now, he had reached a point in his life where *he* was the one craving excitement; actually, anything close to excitement would be welcomed. He thought back on the day with Maya and realized how something about her presence and attention made him feel cared about, and he hadn't been aware of how much he needed that. *Silly*, he thought. He barely knew her. But he understood how it felt to be listened to and have a meaningful conversation. It felt amazing.

It was around five in the afternoon when Royce fell asleep on the sofa, hoping he could catch a little rest before his thoughts forced him awake, which had, unfortunately, been the case in the recent months.

When he awoke, Royce looked at the clock and complained aloud. "Seven o'clock. Well, at least I got two hours of sleep—although I'm sure that will fully ruin any chance of a night's lasting slumber." Suddenly Royce looked at the clock again. It was seven o'clock, alright—*in the morning*. He had slept for fourteen hours! Fourteen glorious hours. But how? *Never mind*, he thought. All that mattered was that it happened. He also realized he'd better kick it in high gear if he was going to make it on time to see the master gardener.

And he definitely was not going to be late for *that*.

When Royce arrived at the cottage, Maya sat quietly on the front porch, sipping coffee.

"Good morning, Royce," she called out cheerfully. "Would you like coffee today?"

"You know, I think I would," he replied with a smile. "Excess sleep got in the way of my morning coffee routine at home, so I'm at a little bit of a caffeine deficit."

Maya smiled and headed into the house to prepare the coffee. When she returned, Royce was sitting comfortably on the chair next to hers as he surveyed the pristine grounds. "You must love it out here," he quietly said. "It's so peaceful."

Maya handed him the dark brown brew and replied, "Remember Royce, peace is anywhere you choose to look for it. It's really not that hard to find, regardless of your circumstances."

Royce couldn't help but edgily react. "Maya, with all due respect, you don't know my circumstances. If you did, you might realize that there's not much opportunity for peace in my life right now."

Maya looked into his eyes compassionately yet firmly and said, "I think you may be mistaken, Royce—even in your situation." Royce reeled from her statement. *Did she know? How could she know? Stew, it must have been Stew that told her. No wonder I keep my life to myself, no wonder I . . .*

Maya's words broke the silence. "Royce, I understand you have gone through a tragedy. No one shared this with me if that's what your astonished look indicates you're wondering. But I feel that I know. Tell me about your wife—if you would, please. I would be honored to listen."

With those soothing words, his shock disappeared, and Royce felt no need to find out how she knew; he just wanted to talk with her about what happened—something he had done little of with anyone at all. But for some reason, he trusted her.

"My wife died three months ago in a car accident, Maya. It was a cool February afternoon when I got the phone call. I had one of my daughters with me, who is fourteen, and my eleven-year-old daughter was staying with family close by. Miraculously, neither of the girls was with her, which was not typically the case. Nevertheless, losing her was horrible, and that day was something that I'm sure has changed me forever. Every day since then feels like my goal is simply to put one foot in front of the other."

The look in Maya's brown eyes was one of empathy, not sympathy. God knows Royce and his daughters had gotten enough sympathy. It seemed like everywhere they went together was punctuated by the locals staring, pointing, or whispering things like, "That's the family. Poor people. I feel so bad for them. I can't imagine."

But Maya was different. She looked into Royce's eyes and quietly said, "Royce, I understand loss very well, as I also have suffered tremendous pain. But I want you to know you are destined for great things in this world. Things you can't even dream of at this point. The agony you have dealt with, and are continuing to deal with, will provide you with the experience you must have for your journey. Remember, there can be no greatness without great struggle along the way. It will take time, but you will get there; trust me."

Even though Royce surprisingly felt a bit of hope from her words, he winced. "I have to tell you; it seems improbable, Maya. Right now, I feel like a shell of a man. I just can't conceive that I could get through this and find the strength that could lead to greatness. In fact, I have a hard time some days thinking I can even find the strength to get out of bed."

Then, he quickly added, "And I worry constantly about my girls. They don't have a mom now, and . . ."

Maya put her hand gently on Royce's shoulder. "Yes, but they have a father. They have a father who will continue to teach them about life and love and faith and the belief that life is not only worth living; it is filled with endless opportunities. Then the day will come, although it seems so far away now, that your girls will marry and have children. Your daughters will use the strength they have learned from this to impact not only their children but many, many other people. Their wisdom and compassion and empowerment will positively influence more lives than you can possibly foresee."

When Maya finished her healing words, Royce nodded in appreciation. "You know, for the first time in months, I feel slightly encouraged. It's as if you knew my story all along, and your words were destined for me. I know that sounds strange, but it's true. Thank you."

Maya leaned forward in her chair, her eyes connecting with Royce in a way that he felt pierced his soul. She smiled softly and then quietly took his hand. "Royce, come with me. I think it's time I shared something with you."

CHAPTER 3

Royce followed Maya around the side of the house to a small garden that encircled a beautiful white gazebo. As they walked up the steps, Royce noticed that everything around the structure was impeccable, just like the rest of her property. The flowers and shrubs surrounding it were inspiring—even breathtaking. As they entered the gazebo, Royce saw four small stone benches, one against each inside wall of the shelter, and a beautiful bronze statue about two feet tall to the side of one of the benches. The statue appeared to be the image of a man and a woman looking toward a star.

Maya seated herself on a bench across from Royce and gave him a moment to enjoy a sip of coffee and take in the surroundings.

"It's beautiful in here, which doesn't surprise me," Royce said. "But the statue . . . I can't describe how it makes me feel. It's magnificent, and I have never seen anything like it. Does it have a story?"

"Yes," she replied without hesitation. That story I'll share with you in due time. But now, sit back and get comfortable. What I'm going to say will come as a surprise to you . . . to say the least."

Royce braced himself as she began her story.

"Royce, I am not sure how you ended up here with me. But I knew you would at some point."

He curiously raised an eyebrow and started to interrupt, but Maya continued.

"As you may have gathered, I'm not from here," she said with a grin.

"Yes, I was going to give you a test to see if you knew that a person should put butter, never jelly, on grits, which is the true test of a Southerner. But I kind of knew you wouldn't pass, so I spared you from that little quiz," he laughed. "So, where *are* you from?"

"India," she replied with a smile. My father was from London, and my mother was from New Delhi, where I was born and raised."

Royce nodded and smiled also. "I've been to both of those cities; England and India are two of my favorite places in the world."

"Interesting," she said. "I've met very few people here who have visited my home country. When I meet those who have, there is always a kindred of spirit."

"Maybe that's why I feel I have a lot in common with you," Royce said.

"Maybe," she replied. "But there's more."

Seeing Royce's quizzical look, she continued. "Royce, you've no doubt heard of Mahatma Gandhi, correct?"

"Of course. In fact, he is one of my favorite historical figures. I have read so much about him and his quest for peace in India."

"Well, Mr. Gandhi was very close to my family. My father was his right-hand person throughout the many years of violent strife in the country, as Mahatma led the Indian people toward independence from the British."

"W-wait," Royce stuttered. "Slow down, Maya. You mean *the* Mahatma Gandhi?"

"Yes, and his name was actually Mohandas to our family, but the followers of Gandhi, and the world in general, knew him as Mahatma, which means 'the great-souled one' in Hindi."

"It must have been incredible to have known him," Royce said, still in shock. "If you asked me which people in history I would most like to have a cup of coffee with and ask questions of them, Mahatma Gandhi would be near the top of my list. As an author and a lifelong student of philosophy, I am intrigued and inspired by Gandhi and the impact he had on the world."

Maya enthusiastically said, "Royce, that is the reason I am sharing this with you. Mr. Gandhi *was* an inspirational person, and when he would come to our home to see my father, I remember his presence and his energy were so soothing yet so powerful. When he was near, you could sense his genuine compassion, and somehow, just being around him made you feel empowered.

"He and his carefully adhered-to principles greatly influenced my father's life, which in turn impacted my life in a way that is difficult to explain; the resulting imprint and transference of positive energy is something I can't begin to describe."

"It almost sounds like he was a . . . a wizard," Royce wondered aloud.

"It's possible," Maya said thoughtfully. "As there are varying degrees of what one would consider wizardry. But one thing is for sure, the precepts he embodied *were* spiritual—maybe even supernatural. They contained power that could, and did, change the world and shape the lives of many prominent leaders of this era: Martin Luther King, Nelson Mandela, and Mother Teresa, just to name a few."

"I'm inspired just hearing this," Royce managed to utter. "I mean, I've read books by Gandhi and about Gandhi, but none of them seem to capture the spiritual essence you're describing. If only he had written these specific principles down, I can't imagine the impact they would have."

Maya paused briefly, then gently reached down and picked up a small, worn, ancient-looking book lying beside her, which Royce hadn't previously noticed. As she turned the book so he could see the faded brown cover, she said softly, "Royce, he actually did."

Royce couldn't believe what he was hearing or seeing. He felt as if everything that had happened over the last two days was a dream.

But it wasn't. As he stared at the book's title, he knew Maya was serious in her claim of the work being Gandhi's. He slowly looked at the mesmerizing words. . .

THE SIX PRINCIPLES OF SACRED POWER

Once again, he had so many questions. But this time, he let Maya lead him.

"Mr. Gandhi, as you may know, spent many years in prison in South Africa. Of course, all of the charges were racially and politically motivated and designed to keep him from carrying on with his work. However, the time in South Africa, specifically in prison, provided him with the isolation and inspiration to begin work on the treatise you see before you. He believed universal principles were available to us all which could overcome any kind of negative force or evil in the world—even those forces that authorities used when attempting to subdue entire populations. He believed that each of us has the capability to accomplish incredible, almost unimaginable feats if we knew how to find the power and tap into it, which is precisely what this book divulges."

Royce was stunned, and Maya could see it on his face. She laughed. "Not what you expected to hear today, I'm guessing?"

"Definitely not. Not today, not tomorrow, not in my lifetime," he said with a smile. "How did he find these universal principles?"

Maya continued. "Mr. Gandhi essentially went back through history, and using every possible translation he could find, reviewed the works of the great spiritual leaders and philosophers of the ages. He then distilled the writings down to a finite number of common principles woven through their literature—six principles to be precise. Those principles became the foundation of his book. It took many years, but he believed when he had finished, the result of compiling all these divine teachings would be insurmountably powerful.

"It turns out he was right. The principles he found in common are, and always have been, available to each of us. But they invariably become inactive—hopelessly buried under layers of anxieties, fears, self-doubt, and discouragement. Mr. Gandhi not only discovered these common denominators; he teaches us how to bring them back to prominence and usefulness in our lives by stripping away the interferences that block their strength.

"Anyone who reads this sacred book and adheres to its principles finds a spiritual power within themselves that one could only call miraculous. Mr. Gandhi's use of the book and its power also undoubtedly changed the course of history in that part of the world."

"This is incredible. I've never seen it, and I've actually never even heard of it," Royce blurted out.

"Aside from conversation with me, you never will," Maya quickly said.

Royce's confusion was written all over his face. "What do you mean?"

Maya continued, "As I said, Mr. Gandhi knew the power of this book. He knew if it got into the wrong hands and the power was misused for malevolent purposes, the results would be potentially horrific. Think about people like Hitler, Pol Pot, Stalin, or Idi Amin and what might have happened if they'd had access to the level of authority this book creates. It could have been catastrophic for humankind. Instead, to minimize the potential of that ever happening, he had only seven copies printed. These were done by a gentleman at a small family-owned book shop in Ceylon, which you know as modern-day Sri Lanka. The publisher was a close friend whom Mohandas had met in his early law school days. Even though they were like brothers, the bookbinder swore himself to secrecy as far as the books were concerned."

"Why specifically seven copies?" Royce asked.

"Mr. Gandhi had six leaders in his organization. He kept a copy of the book for himself, then distributed one copy to each of those leaders, who were, in turn, sworn to the permanent ownership and safekeeping of the books. The only exception was that if one of the leaders should pass away, their copy could be passed on to the person of their choice, and then the same opportunity existed for the next owner. Of course,

Mohandas had complete trust in all of these men, and he knew that whoever they shared the books with, in the event of their demise, would be utterly trustworthy, as would their future owners who inherited copies."

Royce closely followed Maya's incredible monologue. "So, your father, being Gandhi's right-hand person, was entrusted with a book. But . . . how did *you* end up with a copy? Your father? Is he . . ."

"Yes," Maya interrupted. "He died ten years ago. I was so close to him; he graciously left me his copy of the Six Principles."

"Now, I'm starting to get it," Royce said. "Your understanding of my thoughts before I even speak them. Your 'knowing' of the events that happened in my life before you were told. The positive, spiritual energy of this whole place. It's amazing."

"Yes and no," Maya said. "Yes, I know it does seem amazing to you. But as you learn more, you'll understand that the power we have to achieve at a phenomenal level, to overcome any challenge, and to influence the world, has always been within us. We simply need to understand the power, harness it, remove our hindrances, and believe all is possible."

Royce pondered her words. "Maya, when you just said, 'as you learn more,' what did you mean?"

For the first time since Royce met her, Maya's countenance became solemn.

"Although each of the six leaders under Mr. Gandhi, including my father, were sworn to secrecy regarding the existence of these spiritual books, they were expected to live out the message every day. Even without the physical book in hand, the power of the book is so great that people who came in extended contact with one of these ambassadors would become different. They would be connected with an exponentially more empowered, stronger, and compassionate way of living. Those people, in turn, would likewise spread this strength and goodness wherever they went—maybe not even realizing where their new positive influence came from."

"Like a huge, invisible ripple effect," Royce said.

"Yes. Well put," Maya said. "At this point, after all these years, I can almost be sure that you have run into some of these people in your travels who became empowered through this osmosis-like effect—all stemming from these original seven sacred books.

"However, my father's extraordinary service earned him a special gift. He, along with any of the book's heirs which originated from him, was allowed to pass the book on *before* their death, should any extraordinary candidate appear to them."

Royce visibly pondered what was coming next.

"Royce, here's how all of this relates to you," Maya continued. "I know a day will come soon for me to return to India . . ."

Royce immediately resisted. "What? Why? But Maya . . ."

Maya put her index finger gently over Royce's lips. "Even I do not know the exact reason, but I have a strong intuition that there are things I must do there. What's important for you to know is this; I am going to teach you the *Six Principles of Sacred Power* over the next six days. My father would be extremely pleased to have you entrusted with these principles, and I have no doubt Mr. Gandhi would feel the same way."

Royce was flabbergasted as he fumbled his words. "I, um, don't know what to say, Maya. I am so honored, but . . . why me?"

Maya pensively replied, "As I told you before, I am not sure what brought us together. Long ago, I stopped questioning how and why things happen the way they do in my life. I just know they happen for ultimate good, often despite appearances, and they are part of God's plan.

What I also *do* know is that you are the right person to receive this sacred message. With the way events have unfolded in your life and the gift you have to influence the world with your writing, you will be able to authentically share with others how to grow through their trials with renewed strength, faith, and courage not previously understood or believed."

Royce wiped away the tears that he had been trying so hard to fight back. "Thank you, Maya. I won't let you down. I promise."

Maya smiled. "Go home and rest, Royce. Then come back tomorrow morning. We've got a full day ahead of us."

CHAPTER 4

Royce, once again, slept through the night. It was a gift he didn't take for granted after three months of feeling like a zombie every day due to perpetual insomnia. As he quickly dressed, grabbed a bagel, and jumped in the car, he began thinking about the conversations of the previous day. It all seemed so paradoxical to him. Since the accident, nothing seemed to make sense; now, the scenario that should make less sense than anything was starting to make total sense. Although it was something he could not have earlier imagined, he began to believe that Maya's appearance in his life was no coincidence. His mind raced as he thought about the day ahead and the lessons he would learn from this mystical woman.

A few minutes later, he arrived back at Maya's, and this time, the coffee was waiting for him.

Royce smiled and thanked Maya as she led him to an area just off the front porch to begin their talk. "You're very welcome," she said, smiling. "Let's sit here,

Royce. The gardens in the front seem to be especially beautiful today. Some of the flowers in this area are actually varieties that grow back in India also, and I can't help but feel nostalgic when I see them."

"I can imagine. How long have you been in this country, Maya?"

She thought for a moment. "About eight years."

"What made you decide to come here?"

"I suppose that's as good a place to start our discussion today as any," Maya mused. "But would you like your coffee warmed a bit before we start?"

"Sure, thank you."

Maya gracefully reached over and took his cup of lukewarm coffee. She softly clasped it between her two hands, then increased her hold on the mug for several seconds. When she handed the drink back to Royce, Maya smiled. "That should be better."

Royce sat mesmerized as he watched the steam rise from the now piping hot coffee. "Maya, what just happened?"

Ignoring the question, Maya smiled broadly and then politely replied, "Let's begin."

Despite his bewilderment, Royce took a sip of coffee, a deep breath, and then sat back in his seat in anticipation of his mentor's forthcoming words.

Maya seemed to become almost trance-like as she took Royce on a journey he would never forget.

"My father arrived in New Delhi from London years before I was born. He was a young teacher of Philosophy in the graduate school of the university. It was a time when the British were not welcome in India because they were trying desperately to hold onto their "Jewel in the Crown" while the people of India tried to break away. The struggle had been going on for ninety years, dating back to the mid-nineteenth century, and there had been great violence, as you probably know.

"However, even with my father being British, he fell in love with the students and with the Indian people. They reciprocated, and he quickly became one of the most revered professors on the campus. The more my father learned of the injustice and violence perpetrated on the Indian people, the more of an affinity he developed for them.

"During that time, he was introduced to the woman who would eventually become his wife—and my mother. My mom came from the lineage of Queen Laxmibai, the ruler of the Jhansi state of India in the early 1800s and who was possibly the first woman ever to stand up to the British. The queen did that with incredible bravery—eventually dying on the battlefield. My mother was a free-spirited woman who inherited that same spirit of valor and love for India, which my father adored in her. When she met my dad, she was on staff at the university as a translator, and it was, as they say, love at first sight. They courted briefly and then decided they couldn't live without each other, and they were married within the first year. Needless to say, the idea of an Indian woman marrying a Brit was not particularly popular with many people. However, due to the affection and admiration the student body and the faculty had for both of them, it worked out surprisingly well.

"One day, there came word that *Mahatma* Gandhi was scheduled to speak at the school. My father had become increasingly interested in, and sympathetic to, the work Mr. Gandhi was doing with his non-violent methods of defiance. So, he was very excited to attend the lecture that day in New Delhi. Although Mahatma spoke English, my mother was there to help if she was needed during the lecture, and afterward, she was able to get my father a private audience with Mr. Gandhi. My father was elated.

"Even though my dad was British, the connection the two men had was almost instantaneous. The love they had for people, their shared interest in philosophy, and the fact that both men were extremely wise and well versed in current events, galvanized them. It wasn't long after that meeting that my father joined Mahatma in the movement for Indian independence—an incredibly brave thing for my father, or any English person, to do at that time.

"Their relationship grew, and soon, Mr. Gandhi asked my father if he would assume the role of leadership directly under him in his rapidly growing movement. My father accepted, and my mother proudly and wholeheartedly supported the decision, although my parents knew of the inherent danger.

"About two years after my father joined the revolution, I was born. My parents named me Maya, which means *enchantment* in Sanskrit.

"It was also about that time that Mr. Gandhi shared 'the book' with my father.

"Father later told me that when he read *The Six Principles of Sacred Power*, he wept. He said he had immediate clarity that the principles in the book would create a positive final outcome in Gandhi's peaceful revolution against the British, and its capacity for empowering the human spirit would likely change the world.

"Hearing my dad's comments gave Mr. Gandhi the validation he needed, upon which he issued the book to my father, and then to the remaining five leaders. Each of them had similar reactions to my dad's when they read the book.

"The absorption of this sacred book immediately gifted them with unshakable personal powers that are beyond my description, even as I speak now. It was akin to what I believe the Bible calls 'the peace that passes all understanding.' Of course, that power radiated from each of them and spread like wildfire to every person and every group they came in contact with. The result was an unstoppable tidal wave of inspired strength and love across the country.

"From that point, the British never really had a chance."

Maya stopped speaking so Royce could process all he had just heard. He could scarcely get a word out. "Maya, as you can imagine, I have never heard anything like this in my life. Not only did I not know all this happened behind the scenes during that time in India, I had no idea *this* kind of power existed or was available to any of us."

"Yes, it does exist, Royce. God gives us the capability of doing astounding things—supernatural things if you will. Each of those early writers whom Mohandas studied for his publication understood and articulated this understanding in their own ways. But for a variety of reasons, their messages have often been distorted, misused, diluted, or disregarded. Gratefully, Mr. Gandhi had the inspired wisdom to study, distill, and assimilate the powerful, original principles that all of these teachings were based on, so that they could be clearly understood and practically applied," Maya softly said.

In an attempt to lighten the mood, Royce chimed in. "And the results were *magical* if you'll pardon the pun."

Maya smiled. "I guess you could say that."

Like the previous day with Maya, Royce had so many questions, he didn't know where to start. But what he *did* know was that something in him was changing. It was as if he had a small but increasing belief that he would somehow make it through his current challenges and maybe help others do the same thing with their own difficulties.

Royce's encouraging thoughts were interrupted by Maya's gentle voice.

"Royce, here is the first principle you must know . . ."

CHAPTER 5

As Maya began her instruction with the *Six Principles of Sacred Power* on the bench beside her, Royce couldn't help but notice that the book remained closed.

Going immediately into his question mode, Royce asked, "Maya, why aren't you opening the book to teach from?" Maya raised an eyebrow as if she was surprised by the question.

"I hope you don't mind my questions because I know I will have lots of them," he added.

Maya replied, without hesitation. "There are two types of questions, Royce. There are questions of curiosity, and there are questions of interest. Your question was one of curiosity, and I want you to steer away from those as we move forward. Curiosity-based questions show a lack of faith, and there is no room for lack of faith in these teachings. However, I will make an exception for you . . . this one time."

Royce searched for a feeble apology, but Maya kept going.

"To answer your question, I know the book by heart. The book and its message *live* in my heart and in my mind—every chapter, every page, and every word, of which there are 28,342 in this volume, by the way." She smiled.

"I understand," Royce sheepishly replied.

"Good, let's continue. The first principle is. . .

THE PRINCIPLE OF SUPREME GENTLENESS

Royce looked puzzled.

"Gentleness is the overarching theme of this entire work," she said calmly. "It's probably the most misunderstood and underused trait known to humankind. Most people have a connotation of gentleness as one of weakness, and that couldn't be further from the truth. True gentleness is as much of an effective weapon for reaching our desired ends as anything I know of.

"A life which is predicated on this spirit of perpetual softness becomes one that is capable of incredible acts. When gentleness has become a permanent part of our being, the resulting relaxedness gives us a power that we didn't know was available—a power we will then realize had been greatly usurped by anxiety, fear, doubt, and stress before—and now becomes free to be used in mighty ways."

Royce interrupted. "I would venture to guess that most of us live in that realm of constant unconscious tension to some extent."

"That's true," Maya agreed. "The vast majority of people are literally and figuratively holding their breath hoping they can control life's outcomes, all the while unknowingly squeezing out opportunities they never knew were available to them, creating a huge power drain through their tension. But when we have gentleness as our anchor, life doesn't have to be like that, and that's what the early masters were telling us."

Maya persisted, "This trait of supreme gentleness was one that Mr. Gandhi and my father lived out beautifully, and it was energetically transferred to so many people. They were two of the gentlest people I have ever met and were also two of the bravest and strongest people I have ever met. I would offer that only the mentally and spiritually strong are able to be gentle. The gentler one becomes, the stronger one becomes until the point is reached where one is imperturbably serene, resulting in almost unfathomable, unshakable strength. To maintain the soft texture of gentleness during times of ease is one thing, but to be gentle in nearly all times shows a disciplined life with magnificent potential."

Royce rubbed his chin as he let her words sink in. "I never thought of it that way."

"Yes, and again, *most* people don't think of it that way. But this constantly yielding spirit is an effective tool that great spiritual leaders have wisely used in the past. For example, the Christian view of Jesus is one of gentleness, but as you know, he was also undeniably mentally strong," she said.

"Now that I think about that, you're right," Royce said. "Well, of course, that time in the temple with the money changers was an exception. You know, in the New Testament, there's the story about how vendors defiling the sacred temple were chased out by a justifiably angry Jesus."

"I know the story well, Royce," Maya said patiently. "What people often miss in that narrative is the fact that Jesus's actions were carefully chosen. He was a perfect person, and so the perspective of him impulsively losing his temper in the temple was incorrect; that would imply a mistake. Instead, he *chose* to show, by very swift and decisive action, that the money changers' actions were unacceptable and intolerable. That response was symbolic of the fact that there are times when people do not respond to kindness, and so a different course of action *must* be taken. But let me remind you; this is rare, and the route must be navigated with extreme caution. A person who understands the supreme power we've spoken of is very clear on the fact that the firmness or decisiveness required can be delivered most effectively through a calm, non-aggressive spirit. They have likely thought through their forthcoming actions and have determined what they believe will be ultimately effective, with as little short- and long-term collateral damage and repercussions as possible.

"Also, the fact that this type of action by Jesus was recorded so seldom in the entire New Testament is a reminder of how effective a life of gentleness is, and how rarely a deviation from that attitude is needed."

Royce nodded in approval as Maya continued.

"A true life of gentleness is difficult to obtain, but the benefits—as you may understand now—are enormous. It is safe to say that no spiritual warrior can live effectively without this fully embodied trait. The reason this way of living is so challenging is that we are constantly bombarded by stimuli, which beg us to respond—and respond quickly. These stimuli include people, media, communication devices, and much more. All of these distractions are tugging at us and begging us to respond or react in ways that are anything but gentle. 'Better not let someone get ahead of you on the climb up that corporate ladder.' 'Better not let that perceived slight go without defending yourself and your reputation.' 'Better hurry up before you lose your opportunity because it may not happen again.' Those are just a few examples, but there are tens, if not hundreds of similar messages and scenarios we must deal with each day. All of them seem to attempt to pull us into some ego-protecting fight or flight mode, taking us further and further away from a life of gentleness and pure power."

Royce asked, "But what about the potential of us being treated like a doormat if we are consistently gentle?"

"It's a reasonable question, Royce," she said. "But I think what you are really asking is, 'Can we become *too* gentle?' My answer would be no, yet you would have to determine what the right answer is for you.

"What I believe is this; if we are aware of our level of gentleness and we are conscious of the goal we have to be supremely gentle, then we can be aware enough to monitor the results we are receiving along the way. Getting to the point where we have become a 'doormat' as you have suggested, would indicate to me that one has left the realm of placidness and crossed over into either apathy, indifference, or timidity, and that is not at all what we are talking about here. Gentleness may, indeed, be the antithesis of those traits because the gentle person is supremely caring, compassionate, and disciplined. A life at the pinnacle of proactive and persistent yielding—as I saw in my father and Mr. Gandhi—is one which exemplifies grace, patience, kindness, and confidence. It is a life of essentially unflappable peace, regardless of circumstances, and it is capable of extraordinary outcomes.

"Let me conclude with this example, Royce, and I think it is one that will solidify your understanding of the strength a fully actualized life of gentleness brings. I remember it like it was yesterday. Sadly, Mr. Gandhi was assassinated by a fellow Hindu, Nathuram Godse, who didn't believe Gandhi's style of nonviolence and gentleness would be ultimately effective for leading and protecting the country. As he was shot in the chest several times, Mahatma calmly put up his hands in a manner that Hindus do to bless people that approach them. With that instinctive gesture, Gandhi had embodied gentleness to the point that even at that imminent time of death, his peace could not be disturbed. That, I would say, is the ultimate manifestation of the power of gentleness, and it inspired the entire nation and the world. It also terrified his adversaries as they understood this type of peaceful power was potentially much stronger than the weapons they relied on."

"As contradictory as I would have thought this phrase would sound before, I'm starting to see that the strength of gentleness is truly amazing," Royce said.

"Yes, it is. But it is not something to be dabbled in. The power of gentleness becomes fully manifest when it seeps into every aspect of one's life, the way each of the wise ancient teachers in Mahatma's book symbolically showed us. For example, gentleness in our words and tone is critical. When we speak gently to others, we show that we are at peace with ourselves and with them; we have nothing to prove or gain, so we can be fully present and calm. We don't need to speak boastfully; we don't need to speak loudly, and we certainly don't need to speak in a way that insults, demeans, or hurts others. That type of rhetoric drives power away quickly from ourselves and others."

Again, Royce nodded as Maya continued. "There are many other ways we can express gentleness—in our movements, our gestures, our breathing, our eating, our responses to words and situations, and in our life tempo in general. Plus, learning to be gentle with *ourselves* is as important as anything. It may seem overwhelming to think about all these ways to live out gentleness, but suffice it to say, every time we choose gentleness in our thoughts or actions, we are one step closer to being able to habitually incorporate this trait and to benefit from all the power it can offer us."

As Maya concluded her overview, she could see the excitement but also the weariness in Royce's eyes.

"Let's stop here," she said, smiling. "You've done well today, Royce. Tomorrow will be another day of great learning, which will open your eyes to even more possibilities."

Royce couldn't imagine how his eyes could be opened any more than they were that day, but then again, he was also starting to believe that maybe *anything* is possible.

CHAPTER 6

A crisis, as they say, can make you or break you, and for Royce, the jury was still out on what it was doing to him. He awoke with eagerness and optimism about the upcoming day with Maya, but then the familiar, gut-wrenching feelings quickly returned as the painful memories reemerged—just as they had done every morning since the accident.

"It's true that it often takes a tragedy before you understand what's really important in life—and what's not important," he said aloud.

Then something odd happened. Unlike every other morning for the past twelve weeks, as he started the harsh line of unanswerable, painful questions to himself, Royce abruptly stopped as he was gripped by a sudden realization. It was the realization that he was starting to feel a little like his old self. Even, strangely enough, like he was on the path to being a little *better* than his old self.

As he proceeded with his normal morning routine of walking through the house, carrying his morning coffee, he moved slowly as he looked around at all the pictures and the family keepsakes. That day, he saw them *differently*. Items bought for family memories appeared as gifts to be grateful for, not as painful reminders to avoid. The home seemed brighter instead of dark. The house, like Royce, felt more comfortable and peaceful.

Standing in his home looking out the large bay window into the vast stand of oak trees, Royce did something he hadn't done there in a long time; he smiled. Royce Holloway was feeling the transformative power of gentleness.

When Royce arrived at Maya's cottage that morning, he saw her kneeling in one of the front rose gardens, and he couldn't help but notice how beautiful she was in her light yellow sundress, her long hair daintily pulled back. She appeared to be speaking softly to each of the flowers as she caressed their petals. Seeing Royce approach, she gracefully stood to greet him. Royce chuckled. "A little conversation with the flowers today, Maya?" Without hesitation, she responded with a quizzical look. "Of course. Doesn't everyone do that? Besides, I've never had them ask a question out of curiosity, which is refreshing."

Royce laughed. "Okay, you got me on that one." Maya beamed.

"I do have one question this morning," Royce said. "Of course, it's a question of *interest*," he added with a quick grin.

"In that case, fire away," she said with an approving smile.

"How do you keep these grounds so meticulous—with all these thousands of plants and so much property?"

"Thank you for the compliment, Royce. It's a labor of love," she said. "If you remember the first day I met you, we talked about the similarities between gardening and life. I shared with you how my goal is to leave everything more beautiful than I found it, and that's what I have in mind as I work around the property. If anyone comes to see these gardens, I want them to leave feeling like their lives have been made better by being here. The only way that will happen is for me to make sure I put my heart into everything I do."

"I certainly felt my life became better that first day—and I still feel that way every day I'm here," Royce said.

"I'm very glad to hear that, and fortunately, your question fits in beautifully with today's lesson. Let's go to the West Garden and sit; there's plenty of shade, and we have a lot to talk about."

As they walked past the first gazebo, Royce glanced in and once again noticed the small statue. It was a magnificent and unique work of art. As he looked closer, he saw the two figures were so close they seemed connected in an almost spiritual way as they looked toward the lone star, which was so perfectly aligned above and between them. Royce didn't realize he had stopped to gawk at the statue until he heard Maya playfully calling to him. "Let's go, slowpoke. We'll talk about the statue later."

With a child-like grin, Royce said, "Sorry, Coach. I'm coming."

Maya sat cross-legged on the ground in the garden, and Royce frowned as he realized he would need to take the same position. "Royce, sit down. You'll find the lotus position is actually very comfortable now."

"What do you mean, *now?*" Royce asked.

"Now that you understand gentleness," she said with a smile.

Royce slowly eased into the position and waited for the pain to start, but to his surprise, that didn't happen. "I can't believe it," Royce remarked with dismay. "I have never been able to sit like this without my legs feeling like they were going to snap."

Maya laughed. "Royce, as you become increasingly gentle in your manner, you'll find that the deep relaxation which is created will give you more flexibility, more endurance, less stress, and better health in general."

"I think you're precisely right." Royce smiled.

"*Precisely*. Funny you should use that word," Maya said. "Principle number two is this. . .

THE PRINCIPLE OF PRECISION

Royce looked concerned. "I'm not sure I'll do well with this one. I've never been a perfectionist. In fact, I've always thought those were the high strung, 'Type A' kind of folks, Maya."

"While it may seem that I am splitting hairs, perfectionism and precision are two different issues. First of all, perfection is relative while precision is absolute," she countered.

"I don't think I understand," Royce said.

"A child may clean their room and think the finished job is perfect. For them, it may be true. But what would likely be lacking would be the *precision* in the work that was done."

"I . . . think I see," Royce stammered.

Not quite believing Royce had a grasp of the concept, Maya pressed on. "Let me give you another example, Royce. Years ago, I went with my father to visit a Muslim friend of his who had joined the freedom movement but had been expelled by the British for his 'contemptuous' behavior toward them. Quite frankly, they feared his growing influence so much that they kicked him out of the country. He then immigrated to Bangladesh where he lived in a hut by the Bay of Bengal, and where he had taken a vow of simplicity. The dwelling was small, and when my father and I entered, what we saw would not have been called perfect by most people.

"The floor was cracked, the living space was merely adequate, and the walls were sparsely decorated. But the hut had an aura of total peace. Every picture and every decorative item were impeccably placed. You might call it Feng Shui—and that could be true—but the spirit in which everything was done was clearly one of precision. Nothing was out of place. Everything was clean. So, although many people would indeed question the perfection of his house, the *precision* which was present was undeniable. Truly, this man's humble abode was a tranquil, spiritual sanctuary, and the precision of it all reflected his life of simplicity and reverence."

"Simplicity and reverence. I like that," Royce said.

Maya nodded. "Yes, I think those are probably appropriate words. The whole concept of precise activity is based on reverence. When we add an element of precision on top of gentleness, our resulting action could only be described as entering the realm of being reverent or spiritual. As we infuse our actions with precision, whether it is making our bed, washing our car, having a conversation with a friend, playing a sport, or whatever we are doing, we are showing reverence. We're showing reverence to God for giving us the opportunity to do what we are doing. We are showing reverence to ourselves for using our skills and resources to the fullest. And we are showing reverence to other people in the world who may be involved in some way with whatever it is we are doing."

"I followed most of that," Royce said. "But the last part about reverence to other people—I'm not sure I get it."

"I'm glad you asked for clarification on that, Royce, because it's extremely important. Here's an example of what I'm suggesting. If you are having a cup of coffee in the morning, you can drink it in two different ways. One way is to drink it mindlessly and quickly, thinking about what needs to be done in the day ahead, what time you must leave your home to get to your first appointment, and so on. When you finish your coffee, you have not experienced it at all; you have simply consumed it. However, the other way is slowly pouring the coffee, noticing the gentle sound it makes as it fills your ceramic cup, seeing the steam rising, and then enjoying the aroma of the fresh brew. As you drink the coffee, you choose to appreciate the people who picked the beans, drove the trucks to market, operated the machine that ground the beans, and put care into packing the coffee for transport to you, so that you could savor every cup. This type of reverence in your thoughts and actions ensures that you are honoring each aspect of the experiences you are given."

"I get it now!" Royce excitedly said.

"Good," Maya said. "You can also understand that when the elements of gentleness and precision are blended, the result—as the early spiritual masters lived out—is a way of life that is graceful, peaceful, and laser-focused on living harmoniously in the present moment."

"I love that," Royce said. "I can already see how these principles can dramatically improve peoples' lives—including mine. Tell me, Maya, when did *you* learn the principles?"

She pensively responded, "When I was twenty-six. Although I absorbed the principles my father lived out while I was growing up, he never shared the book itself with me until after Mr. Gandhi died. Shortly after that, my father moved with my mother and me to Maldives, off the southern coast of India. He was concerned that staying in India at that time would potentially put his life in danger by the same type of people who attacked Mohandas. My father would share the lessons from the book with me each evening, and I listened in awe the same way you have done. Soon after the lessons were all completed, and I was well-versed in the principles of the entire book, my father became ill, and after a lengthy, difficult few months, he died.

"He left me the *Six Principles* book, as my mother was distraught and did not want anything in the home that reminded her of the movement—including the manuscript. The memories were just too painful for her. I don't think my mother had any idea when she and my father were patriotic, idealistic young people at the university, that the peaceful revolution of Gandhi would grow to the magnitude it did or take the toll on their lives that it did. The stress on her throughout the years of them pushing back so bravely and tirelessly against the opposition was more than my father realized. About six months after my dad died, my mother passed away. She died from a broken heart."

"I'm so sorry," Royce whispered.

"Thank you, Royce. I don't talk about my past with many people, and I certainly don't discuss the details I have shared with you. But I must say, it's quite therapeutic to share with someone who understands and empathizes. Obviously, we now have many things in common." She softly smiled.

"You can say that again," Royce said, smiling back at her.

Maya's inspiring instruction continued for hours. Then at one point, Royce realized he had been sitting in the lotus position for the entire day, with no pain and no thoughts of food. "I can't believe it," he said. If you had told me I could sit this way for so long and be fully engaged—and not hungry—I would have told you that you were crazy."

"Royce," Maya said, "This is what you must understand. What you are learning is changing you. In fact, it already has changed you to a great extent. But one thing that you must take full responsibility for is the belief that you are capable of doing more than you previously dreamed possible. This new belief must permeate your very soul. The spiritual masters that Mr. Gandhi studied, though they were all extremely humble, had the common denominator in their personalities that they deeply *believed* they were equipped for greatness.

They trusted that God had given them the ability to handle tremendous adversity, accomplish great things, and make a powerful difference in peoples' lives. You, too, must believe this, Royce, and it is something I cannot teach you. Do you understand?"

Royce thought for a moment and answered. "Maya, what I know at this point is that there is so much I *don't* know. In fact, I now believe there is a whole other world out there that I don't know. But if I have learned anything, it is this; life is unpredictable. Yet it is precisely that lack of predictability that necessitates us being ready, willing, and able to face those unforeseen challenges as they arise. Through your lessons, I am discovering I have the strength to not only handle the difficulties I am currently facing, but anything else that I must face in the future. Plus, the skills of the mystics which I am being taught by you will help me help others who need it the most. For all of this, I am beyond grateful."

Maya smiled in approval. "You are learning well, Royce. I believe you're now fully prepared to absorb tomorrow's lesson, though I'm afraid it may be a bit painful. Rest well tonight."

CHAPTER 7

Despite Maya's advice to get some rest, Royce slept poorly that night. He was awakened around three a.m. by a terrible dream, and it was so vivid and disturbing, he wasn't able to go back to sleep. So, he simply tossed and turned until sunrise.

In his dream, Royce sat around the kitchen table at a home in New Delhi with a younger Maya, her parents, Mr. Gandhi, and a kind, muscular, handsome Indian man Royce did not recognize, who was sitting next to Maya. As the dream began, the conversation at the table was warm and pleasant. Mr. Gandhi shared stories of his visits to different parts of the world. Maya's parents happily talked of the future of India and of the many people they believed would help shape the country after independence.

But then, something went terribly wrong. Maya's father began arguing with the man sitting next to her. They started yelling loudly at each other in Hindi, and Royce could not understand anything at all. Suddenly, the unknown man unpredictably turned over his chair and stormed out of the room. Maya was left crying and visibly shaken. At that point, Royce awoke in a sweat, with the distinct feeling he had actually been there.

When he arrived at Maya's later that morning and sat on the front porch beside her, she immediately saw the fatigue in his face, but her response was unexpected.

"I see you met Rajiv," she quietly said. "I had the same dream."

"What? What do you mean? Who is Rajiv? Maya, how did you know we had the same dream?" Royce was stunned.

"Let me get your coffee first," Maya calmly replied as she headed to the kitchen.

While Maya prepared the coffee, Royce replayed the scene in his head. *Rajiv. Could that have been the young man sitting next to Maya at the kitchen table? But who was he, and how did she know?*

His thoughts were interrupted by Maya's gentle steps approaching him with a fresh cup of java.

"Here, sip on this," she said.

Royce took the coffee and nodded as Maya began speaking.

"Royce, when two like-minded people are doing the kind of deep spiritual work you and I are doing together with the book, the power generated can often be phenomenal. Sometimes the effects surprise even me. For example, one of the phenomena that may result is entrainment of thoughts."

Royce froze. "You mean we can read each other's minds?"

"More like our thoughts are often the same—including last night's dream."

"I suppose I'm reaching the point in our discussions where nothing surprises me," Royce said as he shook his head. "But . . . can you tell me about the dream? Who is Rajiv?"

"Today was the day I was going to discuss this with you," Maya calmly replied, taking a deep breath. "Which is likely why we both experienced the vision."

Maya continued. "The man in the dream, Rajiv, was to be my husband."

Royce's shock was evident. "Your *husband?*"

"Yes," she replied delicately.

"There was a period during the revolution when my father was extremely concerned for the safety of my mother and me. So much so that he hired two bodyguards—one for each of us. Rajiv, my guard, was ten years older than me, but we had so much in common it seemed there was no age difference at all. The more we were near each other, the more our feelings for each other grew, until our relationship reached the point where we both believed we were destined to be together. Rajiv was ready to propose to me, but we feared my father would not approve; he had always warned me to watch out for older men. Plus, when Rajiv applied to be my bodyguard, he assured my father that he did not mix business with pleasure, so my father felt confident nothing would develop between us. Fate had other plans.

"After two years of secretly seeing each other and growing increasingly in love, Rajiv convinced me that he should tell my father. One Sunday afternoon, Mr. Gandhi had been invited to our home for lunch, and my father asked Rajiv to join us as a thank you for the job he had done. I sat to Rajiv's left, as you saw in your dream. You also saw that to Rajiv's right was my father. The mood was light, and Rajiv was having a wonderful conversation with my father. I suppose their connection that day led him to believe that the time was right to share our news."

Maya paused. "But he was wrong. So wrong. Despite being the kind soul that he was, my father went into a rage. It was the only time in my life I ever saw him like that. The two men began arguing, and despite Mr. Gandhi attempting to calm the situation, the argument escalated. Finally, in an angry, impulsive reaction, Rajiv turned his chair over and proceeded to storm out the door. All I could do was cry."

"Maya, I'm sorry. I . . . I don't know what to say."

"Neither did I," Maya said quietly.

"I could not marry Rajiv without my father's blessing, and Rajiv knew that. After the day at our house, Rajiv never returned. I received a letter several days later from him."

With that, Maya reached in the side pocket of her sundress and pulled out a tattered, yellowed piece of paper and began reading.

"My Dearest Maya,

Never did I dream this day would come. When God brought you into my life, it was as if I had found not only the woman of my dreams but the woman who would surely be every man's dream. Every moment I have been with you, I have felt the need to pinch myself, wondering how I could ever be blessed with such a beautiful, kind, courageous person like you.

"But for a reason maybe we shall never know, the heavens have decided that our life together is not to be. My heart breaks as I write these words knowing that I will not see your smile, feel your touch, and hear your voice, as we now go through life apart from each other.

"Please know that although I will not be with you, I long for the day when India will be free, and you and I will see each other again. Until that day, know how deeply I love you.

Rajiv"

Royce saw the pain in Maya's eyes. "Yes, I now see even more clearly that you understand loss, Maya," he said gently. "Although death is unthinkably hard, so is a horrible separation like you went through. I am so sorry."

Royce instinctively reached out and wrapped his arms around the tearful Maya. At that moment, there was no teacher, and there was no student. Instead, there was simply a connection between two souls who understood the deep sadness that must often enter this otherwise joyous event called life.

After several moments, Maya slowly pulled away and looked Royce in the eyes. "Thank you, Royce. Even after all these years, the pain seems to unexpectedly return."

She wiped her eyes and managed a smile. "Now, I think you and I still have some things to talk about, don't we?"

"Yes, I guess we do," Royce softly agreed.

Maya seemed to stoically put her emotions behind her as she looked at Royce, and calmly stated the third principle. . .

THE PRINCIPLE OF
UNSHAKABLE GENEROSITY

"In the profound spiritual realm we are dealing with, Royce, authentic generosity is not an act but a lifestyle. You've heard the phrase 'give until it hurts'?" Royce nodded. "Well, when the level of generosity I'm speaking of is reached in a person's life, generosity gives them no discomfort at all because it is such an integral part of who they are at their core. In other words, if one is living out this degree of generosity, their way is one of constant giving."

Royce thought for a moment. "So, this type of giver doesn't worry about running out of money?"

"That is correct, but this is by no means just about money, Royce," Maya responded quickly. "The point is to give when there is a perceived need. To fully generous people, money is simply one small piece of the puzzle, and many times, money is *not* the best thing to give. But if it is, they give without fear of there not being enough to go around.

"By the way, in case you are wondering, unshakably generous people do not give expecting anything in return. If they receive a thank you or some kind of acknowledgment, they are quick to respond, but once they have given whatever was needed, their work is done, and it's time to move on. No applause necessary."

"What are other ways to express generosity?" Royce wondered aloud.

"Generosity with time, with talent, with listening skills, with empathy, with sincere compliments, smiles, the options are almost limitless," Maya said. "Looking back at each of the mystics Gandhi studied, their lives were shining examples of this. They also knew when you implement the elements of gentleness and precision, and then layer on generosity, the result is a substantial increase in peace, joy, and fulfillment."

"I will have to say, some of my happiest times have been when I was doing for others," Royce said.

"Yes, it is a powerful law of human nature, and one the masters understood well. For example, they believed a generous spirit made them invulnerable to anger, insults, and negativity in general, and I wholeheartedly agree," Maya added.

"How's that?" Royce asked with a perplexed look.

"As I mentioned, generosity was embedded so deeply in them; it's really the only response they had. Good deeds and words toward them were appreciated. Bad words or deeds toward them were ignored, learned from, or redirected. They seldom took anything personally because they knew if they reacted angrily, defensively, or contradictorily, it weakened them. So, if situations like this presented themselves, the wise leaders simply chose not to participate."

"Pretty smart if you ask me," Royce quipped.

She continued. "Yes, the word 'smart' you selected is quite appropriate. The ancient teachers also realized that generosity was a wise path for another reason."

Royce leaned in as Maya kept going. "Most people don't stop to think that generosity is an act of faith and that generous acts strengthen our belief systems. When we give, we are choosing to believe that our wants and needs will be taken care of out of God's unlimited abundance. Those who choose to hold on or refrain from giving are asserting their belief that they will not have enough, so in their minds, there is *certainly* not enough to give away. This fearful "scarcity" mindset is not only disempowering; it becomes a self-fulfilling prophecy. Giving inspires belief, hope, and compassion and opens the door for more of those things to come into one's life. Absence of generosity, on the other hand, being a manifestation of a deficit-oriented mentality, creates more affirmation of distrust, disempowerment, and insecurity of future needs being met."

"Essentially, you get more of what you give—or don't give," Royce said.

"Well said. Generosity is quite a powerful concept."

As had become the pattern, their conversation went on for hours, but the Georgia sun was especially hot that day.

"Royce, how about let's go inside for some lunch? I have fresh vegetables from the garden, and I've made some lemonade also," Maya said.

"That sounds great," Royce replied. "I'm starving."

Lunch provided the opportunity to talk about other aspects of life, and Maya kicked the conversation off as they dug into the fresh corn, tomatoes, and beans she had prepared.

"Royce, have you always been a writer?"

"Well, in my previous life, so to speak, I was a professional tennis player," he said, smiling.

"Really? Fascinating. Is that when you visited India?" Maya asked.

"Yes, and as I mentioned before, it was without a doubt one of my favorite countries," he said. "It was an enchanting, mystical place."

"What cities did you travel to when you were there?" Maya asked.

"Bombay, New Delhi, Madras, and Bangalore, to name a few."

"Mmm, wonderful places. The names are still melodic to me." She smiled. "My uncle lived in Bangalore."

"The nation's refrigerator, I believe it is called, due to the slightly cooler climate," Royce said.

"Bravo again." Maya beamed as she clapped her hands. "I am impressed with your knowledge of my country."

Royce smiled bashfully.

"What other countries did tennis take you to?" she asked.

"Now you're asking me to dig deep; it's been a while," Royce chuckled. "Let's see; Switzerland, Bermuda, Morocco, Australia, New Zealand, England, and Brazil were wonderful places, and then there were quite a few others I would just as soon forget. It was a great way to see the world but a tough way to make a living." Then it was Royce's turn. "Maya, how did you end up here in Georgia?"

Maya paused. "When my mother and father passed away, I left Maldives and returned to India for two more years. I even became involved in politics on the national level, as I had developed relationships through my father with many high-ranking officials. But I left the political world after the corruption I saw was finally too much to take, and one day I realized I had nothing left to keep me in India. Ironically, I began to understand how my mother felt once my father died as far as wanting to get away from any reminders about the revolution. I, too, needed to get away, but from *everything*."

She continued, "I took a year and traveled the world, seeing many beautiful places and visiting some of my parents' old friends in countries like Peru, South Africa, Italy, Thailand, and Sweden. I also came to the States and met some people who told me about this part of the country and the slow pace. I found this piece of land and fell in love with it, so I decided to stay."

"We seem to have another thing in common," Royce said. "Traveling the world. But do you ever miss your homeland?"

"Ah Royce, do you remember when I told you on that first day that wherever I go, that's my home?"

"Certainly," Royce said.

"I sincerely meant that. I have found that memories make excellent servants but terrible masters. So, I make it a habit not to look back very often—especially when it's not the direction I am planning on going," Maya said with a grin.

"It's a good reminder," Royce said as he reached for another serving of beans. "Sometimes, I get hung up on memories, and I beat myself up a little bit. Well, no, actually a *lot*."

Maya thought for a moment and then commented. "Royce, when we talked about gentleness, you remember, I said being gentle with *ourselves* is a high priority?"

Royce nodded.

"Well, it's really the number one priority when it comes to mastering that trait. It's difficult to fully engage in the present beauty surrounding us until we disengage from the baggage of the past. When it comes to feeling guilty about decisions we previously made, gently and sincerely reminding ourselves *we made the best decisions we could with the information we had available at the time* is a powerful way to accelerate the disengagement. It can become a mantra to repeat each time you find yourself heading to a dark place in your mind."

Royce let her words sink in and then replied, "I needed to hear that. Being a single parent is new territory for me. It seems like I am getting advice from everyone—some well-intended, and some, well . . . I have my doubts about it. I often feel misunderstood, unappreciated, and I feel pulled in so many directions. Quite frankly, I'm not certain my decisions *are* right sometimes, but I'm really trying hard."

Maya replied quickly, "Getting to the point where you can rest in that uncertainty is important, Royce. None of us always knows the direction we should take, yet the surest route to disempowerment and helplessness is becoming dependent on the opinions of others; we must find the way for ourselves. There will *always* be people willing to give us plenty of advice on what should be done or what ought to have been done in difficult situations. The highly evolved person simply listens, thanks them for their input, and then chooses the path which they feel is best. That takes confidence, patience, and courage, but it is the way of the gentle warrior, Royce, which you are becoming."

Royce let out a huge sigh of relief. "Maya, once again, that was exactly what I needed to hear. Your words make me feel like all the trials, as painful as they have been, are preparing me for things in life that I couldn't be ready for otherwise. I am seeing how the principles which the great ones lived out can also help me achieve a level of self-mastery and personal power that I didn't understand before."

"You're right, Royce. We don't understand why things happen in our lives—at least I know I don't. But as I said, there is a plan that we must trust is working for our ultimate good. When we fully embrace that plan with a gentle heart, precise efforts, and a generous spirit, we have laid the groundwork for greatness to emerge."

"But," she added as she changed the subject, "there are more principles to cover, which we will continue doing tomorrow. Finish your lunch, and let's go back outside. I have something else I want to discuss with you today."

Royce and Maya sat under a huge spreading oak tree for their afternoon session. It provided the perfect amount of shade from the hot sun, and it also allowed for a beautiful view of the stream, which ran quietly through the back part of the sprawling acreage.

"The lunch was fantastic, Royce said. "The vegetables were so fresh. Are you . . . a vegetarian?"

Maya raised her eyebrows, and Royce realized he had chosen his question poorly. "Um, a curiosity question, huh?" he gulped.

She nodded. "Royce, I am a person. I am a *person* who happens to choose to abstain from eating meat. I am also a person who happens to choose Hinduism as my religion. I am also a person who enjoys gardening. These are all things I do, not who I am."

Royce knew his schooling wasn't over, even though Maya had a slight smile on her face. She continued, "There is a distinctly different energy when questions are asked out of curiosity, Royce. It's important when someone is on a spiritual quest, like you are, for your questions to have no hint of anything besides compassion and a search for meaning and truth. They should be questions that will create a positive mutual flow of energy between the people conversing. Answers to questions asked out of curiosity are typically filtered by the questioner through lenses of preconceived ideas or bias and usually do not support mutually beneficial, increased understanding. For example, your question about my choice of vegetarianism is going to be filtered through your interpretations of what that type of diet is about and what type of people choose to partake in it. However, having been a person who has chosen this lifestyle for as long as I can remember, I can guess my reasons for this are different than most people you know who choose vegetarianism. At best, a curiosity-based inquiry can give the questioner a little personal information they didn't have before, but it can also put the answerer on the defensive, feeling the need to justify or clarify their position. It's all just so unnecessary and potentially draining for one who is seeking spiritual growth."

Maya finished by saying, "Royce, if it still feels like this is a minor distinction, remember this; on your new journey, what most feel are minor distinctions are actually places where the pure gold lies. Your path is now one of precision, and this also means precision in your words, including questions. Each question should be preceded by asking yourself, 'What's my motive?' Once you determine the motive is noble and the question is necessary, continue. Otherwise, realize and act on the understanding that it is a question better left unasked.

That was the way of the spiritual greats, and it should now be *your* way."

Royce nodded and sheepishly added, "I think I've got it, Coach."

Maya smiled and changed her direction, and a compassionate yet serious look came over her.

"Now, I have a question for you, my friend."

Royce braced himself, wondering where this conversation was about to go.

"What is the fear you carry, Royce?" He was stunned. He knew Maya's tone well enough to know this had nothing to do with the accident, yet he feebly attempted a deflection.

"You mean, what do I worry about for my future now that things have changed in my life so much?"

Maya shook her head and smiled. "From the second day I spent time with you in the garden, I sensed you were burdened by something—something that had nothing to do with what happened in February. I don't ask leading or probing questions, Royce, so whether you choose to answer is up to you. I assure you, my motive is pure, and I feel that your answer and our subsequent discussion may be both healing and empowering to you."

Royce felt incredibly vulnerable, and even though vulnerability wasn't typically an area he liked to wade into, he felt—no, he *knew*—this time was a necessary exception.

He looked into Maya's awaiting eyes and began, "As much as people seem to see me as a success, I feel sometimes like . . . a fake." Royce expected to see surprise—maybe even disappointment—come over Maya when she heard his words, but she remained serene and attentive. He continued, "By most peoples' standards, I have achieved what many would think of as triumph beyond their wildest dreams, but I often feel so undeserving. Maybe I think I have just been lucky or even privileged, but whatever it is, at times, I feel like somewhere, someone is going to expose me and take everything away."

With a caring, nonjudgmental tone in her voice, Maya asked, "When did this sentiment start?"

"I don't know," Royce said. I suppose it has always been there to an extent. Sometimes it's worse than others."

Maya gently placed her hands on his and compassionately asked, "Share an example with me, Royce. Tell me of a time you remember feeling this way."

Royce seemed to drift off into deep thought, and he began his story. "I was twenty-five, competing in North Africa on the tennis tour. It was Tunisia, to be precise. It was so hot—maybe 100 degrees Fahrenheit, and it was the finals of the tournament. At the time, Tunisians hated Americans, so the fans weren't too fond of me. They booed me every time I won a point and cheered every time I made a mistake. Somehow, I reached a match point, which means all I needed to do was win one more point, and I was the tournament champion. The crowd was screaming against me, the sweat was pouring off of me, and at that moment, I felt a panic sweep over me like I had never felt. *Who am I to win this tournament on the other side of the world? Had I worked hard enough? Had others sacrificed more than me? What was a small-town boy like me even doing on this court with such great players?*

"The point began. Back and forth, the ball traveled over the net. Finally, there was my opportunity—the shot was so easy. I made it a million times in practice, but that strong sense of doubt and fear came over me right as I hit the ball, and my shot landed out of bounds. My heart sank as the Tunisians screamed their delight at my mistake. Before I knew what had happened, I had lost the game and then lost the match. As I sat on the sidelines afterward, I angrily and sadly realized that the loss was not because the player was better, but because *I had beaten myself.* I had confirmed my fears that I was not worthy of the victory."

Maya saw the pain Royce was in, and she squeezed his hands a little tighter. "I'm sorry."

Tears appeared in Royce's eyes, and Maya tenderly wiped them away. Royce sat up straight as if to assert to her the pain wasn't *that* bad . . . but it was. They both knew it.

"Where else does this type of thinking show up in your life, Royce?" Maya quietly asked.

Without hesitating, he replied, "My writing. I have multiple bestsellers, yet I often wonder if I deserve them. I also sometimes doubt I am worthy of the adoration from my fans."

Maya paused, and a pensive yet understanding look came across her face.

"Imposter Syndrome," she emphatically said. Royce looked perplexed. "What are you talking about? Are you saying I really am an imposter, Maya?" Her response was swift. "Just the opposite. *You* are saying you are an imposter. That is called Imposter Syndrome, and it affects probably seventy percent of the population at some point. However, it's most prevalent in the lives of super achievers like you."

"I've never heard of it," Royce added.

"When someone is affected by Imposter Syndrome, they convince themselves their success is simply due to luck or being dealt some supremely good hand by fate. They rationalize that they don't deserve what they have gotten because they aren't particularly worthy recipients, in their own opinion—most often a false opinion—as in your case. It creates so much personal pressure that it becomes nearly impossible for them to savor their success—even for a short time."

Royce blurted, "But what can I do, Maya?"

Maya tenderly placed her fingers on Royce's temples. "Close your eyes and do not open them until I tell you."

Royce nodded and felt himself drifting off into a semi-conscious state as he closed his eyes and savored Maya's soft touch.

The next thing Royce knew, he was on a tennis court near the ocean under a magnificent blue sky. "Where are you now, Royce?" Maya asked, speaking quietly.

Without opening his eyes, he murmured, "The island of Bermuda—it's so beautiful."

"What are you doing, Royce?"

Royce quickened his words. "I just won the national championship here—the people were so kind, and the experience was amazing. I feel like a hero."

"Very good, Royce." Maya massaged the sides of his head and then pressed in on his temples again with utmost care. "Where are you *now*, Royce?"

"I'm sitting home reading a letter from a woman who read one of my books."

"What does the letter say, Royce?"

He appeared to be reading from the letter word by word as he said aloud:

"Dear Mr. Holloway,

I've never written to an author before, but I felt led today to write to you.

For a lot of reasons, I have struggled with feeling inadequate and hopeless most of my life. Seeing therapists, seeking counsel from friends and family, even taking prescribed medication, seemed to be ineffective. I have to say; I was at my wit's end. In fact, I was strongly considering ending my life. However, someone gave me a copy of your book, and when I read it, something inside me changed. I really don't know why, but I somehow felt capable, strong, even happy. It has been months now, and I reread your book often. Every time I do, I feel myself becoming more and more inspired and confident. I truly believe now that my life has a purpose, and I believe I have great days ahead. I just wanted to tell you how grateful I am. Please don't stop writing. Your work makes a difference.

Sincerely,

Autumn E."

"Open your eyes, Royce."

When he did, he saw Maya looking at him, smiling broadly. Upon seeing this, Royce smiled also.

"That was . . . I mean . . . you are . . . incredible, Maya. I don't know how it happened, but I was *there*. It was unbelievable."

"Unbelievable is no longer in your vocabulary, Royce," Maya smiled. "Your life is all about belief. What you saw in your mind were examples of successes you have had in the past, which you have ignored or lost focus on. There are many, many more places I could take you to refresh your memory of past victories. However, that is *your* job now. I helped you begin to remember how capable and effective you really are, but it is up to you to continue to put any perceived failures you have dwelled on in perspective. Each setback only prepared you for greater success in the days ahead. You must stand up to your Imposter Syndrome and remind it that there is no imposter here—only a powerful person choosing to make a difference in the world by using everything that happens as a means to a greater end."

Royce was speechless. Even though he understood the concept of "entrainment" as she had shared with him, he couldn't fathom what had just happened. But he was so grateful that it did.

Maya quietly advised Royce, "Now, I think you will sleep well. Go home and come back tomorrow. We have much more work to do and not much time."

As she h
opened h
friend

CHA...

There were no bad dreams for Royce that night. He awoke refreshed and excited about the upcoming lesson he would learn. He could feel all of the previous teachings sinking into his actions as he went through his morning routine. Gentleness, precision, and generosity seemed to be increasingly present in everything he did, and he noticed how life had become more enjoyable in a number of ways. Each day with Maya seemed to provide him with not only more knowledge but an increasingly rejuvenated spirit and a calmer way of handling the daily difficulties he faced. One thing that troubled him, however, was her comment right before he left the evening before. "We have much more work to do *and not much time . . .*"

Royce tried to put it out of his head as he got in his car and headed down the road to Maya's house. When he arrived, he saw Maya sitting quietly and still on the front porch with her eyes closed.

heard him walk up the steps, Maya slowly
er eyes and greeted Royce. "Namaste, my
Have a seat, and I will get us some coffee."

Royce smiled and sat in a chair on the porch as
Maya stood up from her pose and headed in to get their
morning brew. When she returned, she sat in a chair
beside him.

"You used the term 'Namaste' to welcome me a few
moments ago," he said. "I've heard that greeting many
times, but I've never known what it meant."

Maya smiled and replied, "It is a Sanskrit term
which means, the divine in me bows to the divine in
you. It's a greeting, which also has a tone of reverence
to it."

Royce laughed nervously. "The *divine* in me? Well,
I know we talked about not giving in to Imposter
Syndrome, but I'm not sure I could convince myself
that I'm divine."

Maya smiled again. "Royce, I must admit, I'm
far from an expert on Christianity, but if I remember
correctly, the Bible has a verse which states, 'The
kingdom of God is within you,' correct?"

Royce thought for a moment. "Well, I guess you're
right. I've just never thought of it like that."

"I think if you go back and review the New
Testament of the Bible, you'll find there are many
passages that support not only the fact that we have a

divine power within us, but which also support what we have talked about over these last few days."

"I've thought about that," Royce said. "In fact, I've thought a lot about faith in general since I've been here with you. Even though we are of different religions, I feel so many of our beliefs and values are similar."

"I wouldn't disagree. Who knows, if you had been born in New Delhi, you might have been a Hindu." Maya smiled.

"And if you were born in Georgia, you could have been a Southern Baptist like me," Royce said with a grin.

"Touché!" Maya laughed.

She continued. "Let me ask you something, Royce. How has your faith been affected by the crisis you went through?"

Royce rubbed his chin thoughtfully and then, with the slightest hint of a smile, asked, "Is that a question of interest or curiosity?

"I practice what I preach, as you say here in America. I always check my motives before asking a question." Maya winked.

"Well, in that case," Royce began, "I'll tell you, because it *has* been on my mind—not only as I have spoken with you this week, but over the last three months.

Maya nodded with an understanding smile as Royce continued.

"Before the accident, I think I was on autopilot with my religion. I dutifully accepted what I was taught, I read my Bible diligently, and I made sure I dotted my I's and crossed my T's when it came to the expectations people had of me."

Maya looked puzzled. "Dotted your I's and crossed your T's? I'm afraid I'm unfamiliar with that one—could you translate that into Hindi?" she said with a mischievous smile.

Royce laughed. "Sorry. It means I was pretty much a perfectionist when it came to fulfilling my church and religious duties."

Maya grinned. "Got it."

"After the accident, it's not as if my faith shrank. In fact, many people, when they go through a tragedy, ask, 'why me?' But I did not, strangely enough—even though I was devastated. What *did* happen was that I lost the need to be doing what I perceived as all the "right" things to find heavenly acceptance or to make God happy. I began to simply live my life and live out my faith in a way that I chose, with the values and beliefs I have learned and that I hold so dear. I let go of the need to feel bound to the standards, judgment, and mandates of others. My Christian faith grew to a new level as my rote dependency on religious doctrine and instruction diminished, and the practical application of the Scriptures became even more evident to me."

Maya was listening carefully. "Royce, what specifically caused the shift in your thinking?"

He pondered the question. "It's difficult to explain. I think I felt as if a huge, illusionary safety net I believed was there was pulled out from under me. Soon after, I quit living a life of believing my religious works were creating some kind of lucky charm, and I started living a life of pure and simple faith that everything in my life has a purpose, with nothing else required of me."

Maya again nodded. "It sounds to me as if your letting go of what *seemed* to be spiritually important, allowed you to grasp what *truly* is important."

"I couldn't have said it better, Maya," Royce said with a smile.

Maya thanked Royce for sharing, and as she did so well, shifted into the day's lesson on the Six Principles. "Royce, I think you will find that what we are going to discuss from Mr. Gandhi's work today will tie in nicely to what we just talked about. It is one of my favorite principles . . .

The Principle of Unending Appreciation

Royce listened carefully as Maya continued. "Most people go through life waiting for things to happen, which they would classify as 'good' before they express any kind of appreciation. One who is spiritually mature knows differently. They know that there is good inherent in virtually everything, everyone, and every experience in life; it is simply up to them to proactively find that goodness.

Royce gestured a subtle thumbs up and commented, "Gratitude. I love this."

Maya nodded. "Gratitude is something that people have come to casually believe will get them what they want if they just affirm it enough. However, it's a dangerous way of looking at appreciation. That type of thinking is more of a thinly veiled attempt at controlling life and manipulating the spiritual laws for self-serving ends. It's not only fundamentally selfish; it's ineffective. That is a mindset which is focused on getting rather than giving, and the universe won't be fooled."

Royce was intrigued as she continued. "Genuine appreciation or gratitude is based on the simple concept of recognizing and offering thanks for what one has been given without expectation of some future benefit. It is completing the circle of good by humbly giving deference to a power greater than ourselves; no strings attached.

"True gratitude—much like generosity—is an indicator of faith."

Royce was mesmerized. "I can see how powerful that would be. But what is the circle of good you just mentioned?"

Maya quickly responded. "This is where the unending aspect of *unending* appreciation comes in. Energy in life is in constant movement, constant flow if you will. It's always stirring around, creating, and recreating. When we live in never-ending appreciation, we are allowing the flow to continue—we are keeping the energy moving, as opposed to allowing it to clog up anywhere. As our state of being evolves into one of constant or unending gratitude, we allow life to unfold naturally, effectively, and we then trust everything is happening in the best interest of all—a circle of good."

Royce nodded. "So, when a person isn't grateful, the cycle is incomplete?"

Maya shrugged. "I guess you could say that. Essentially, the energy becomes stagnant or low-level. Have you ever been around someone who seldom has any words of appreciation and unfailingly looks for ways that life has been unfair to them?"

Royce smiled. "Oh, yes. I know a few of those folks."

"Well," she said, "What you probably notice when you are around them is that there is an uninspiring air of heaviness they exude."

Royce quickly agreed. "Exactly. I've never heard it described like that, but yes, it's a perfect description."

Maya continued. "That lack of lightness is due to the fact that their energy is stale. Their personality has basically been inundated with heavy traits of ingratitude, pessimism, and lack, and it's bottled up inside of them with no place to go. The circle of good is disconnected, and therefore ineffective—for themselves and others around them."

Without realizing he was speaking aloud, Royce said, "Wow! I never knew appreciation had that kind of depth to it."

Maya shook her head. "It's unfortunate and unnecessary for people to live a life of ingratitude. They have no idea what is available and what this unappreciative mindset is doing to them and those they love. Living in the realm of gratitude can change everything. For example, when it comes to dealing with difficulties in life, once we start learning to find goodness or gifts embedded in each situation we encounter—instead of complaining and criticizing, we start understanding bad is, more often than not, actually a comparative term."

Royce's sudden change of countenance seemed to indicate he wasn't quite sold on that. "Surely you're not saying that everything that happens to us is a good thing, Maya."

Maya instantly and firmly responded. "Of course not. If that were the case, we would lose all feelings and emotions except for happiness; and we know that isn't reality. What I am saying is this; there is a perfectly designated place for everything and everyone in our lives, but we aren't always able to see it. It's similar to the way pieces of a puzzle all fit together to form a beautiful final picture. We don't initially know where all the pieces should go, but as we work through the puzzle, we start getting more clarity. With a mentality of unending appreciation, even though we will still feel pain, disappointment, and all sorts of emotions, we begin to understand that there are powerful lessons available to us in even the direst of situations—although it may take time to see them."

Royce nodded. "So, it doesn't mean we *should* or *will* be happy about everything that happens, but instead, we can be assured that through it all, there is a universal interconnectedness, and we can be grateful that there is a plan and a purpose. Even though we can't always see that purpose immediately, something will invariably come from our pain and challenges, strengthening our lives where and when we need it the most."

Maya applauded the comment. "Well said, Royce. When we learn to be grateful for life as it is presented to us, when we give up resistance, we allow space for even better things to potentially come into our lives. But remember, effective appreciation is ongoing and unending. We don't choose to pull thankfulness out of our pocket for those times we decide to shortsightedly label as good, or times we choose to label as bad. What the spiritual giants showed us was that *gratitude is a way of life.* When we start understanding and embracing that, we shift into a different dimension. We better see how things fit together, and so we become more peaceful, more courageous, and more loving. We look at life's ups and downs through different lenses, and we begin to fully trust the wisdom of the bigger, better plan at work for our ultimate good. But I will also add, this is difficult spiritual work for the vast majority of people—so difficult that they do not even attempt it."

Royce followed closely. "It's very interesting to me. I have written about gratitude for a long time, but I didn't understand the roots of its power. Now, more than ever, I can see the width and depth of the effectiveness of this trait."

Maya replied, "Unending appreciation was deeply ingrained in the lives of the spiritual greats. They were practicing it thousands of years before today's self-help authors began espousing its benefits—no offense to you." She smiled. "They also understood that this type of gratitude was contagious, and so they wove it into every opportunity they had available to them. As you can imagine, when unending appreciation is layered on top of gentleness, precision, and generosity, the resulting momentum created is like a tidal wave—nearly unstoppable."

"Nearly?" Royce said.

"At this point, *nearly* is the correct word. We still have two more principles to go—where the *real* magic begins to happen," Maya said with a tone of intrigue. "However, we will need to stop today's lesson here, although it is early. I have pressing issues to deal with, which I have only today become aware of, and so I'll let you go home and think about what you've learned up to now. Come back tomorrow, and we'll continue."

As he agreed, the thoughts started running through his mind. *Pressing issues? What could she be talking about? Where—and why—was she going?*

It was odd. Royce couldn't understand his reason for questioning her motives. What were these feelings he was having? Surely, he wasn't feeling jealous . . . was he? After all, he'd only known her five days, and their lives were so different—and she was older . . . much older. But he had come to feel that something about her—maybe *everything* about her—was enchanting to him, and the time they spent together was nothing short of dreamlike.

Royce managed to bring all the thoughts racing through his mind to a quick halt. He wanted to do exactly what Maya asked of him—go home and ponder all he had learned up to that point.

And there was a *lot* to ponder.

CHAPTER 9

When he got home, Royce plopped down on the couch and began thinking about the recent whirlwind days of his life.

Although it had been less than a week—which seemed impossible—Royce knew the *Six Principles of Sacred Power* were incrementally, and permanently, transforming him. Before this week, he wondered how he would carry on. He wondered what each day would bring and where he would be even a month from now. As a writer who loved making peoples' lives better through his encouraging words, he had come to feel indescribably discouraged and alone. Gratefully, there were some big-hearted friends and family who non-judgmentally assisted him and the children. Yet he continued trying to shake the critical words of those people who were more than willing to tell him what *they* would do if they were in his shoes.

But they weren't in his shoes.

He often wondered whose shoes *he* was in. No one could have prepared him for this ordeal, but he knew that the journey was his alone, and he must take it.

Regardless of the naysayers, the armchair quarterbacks, and the folks with 20/20 hindsight, Royce knew holding it together for himself and his family was up to *him*. Which, quite frankly, scared him to death.

Then the day of Stewart's infamous phone call encouraging him to meet the "Master Gardener" happened.

At that moment, Royce felt a sense of panic as he thought, *What if I hadn't taken the phone call? What if I chose not to meet Maya? What if I had not come back after that first day in the garden?*

But he did. Maybe it was coincidental; maybe it was fate, or maybe it was just plain luck, but he was grateful—mighty grateful. The traits of gentleness, precision, generosity, and unending appreciation were ones that he always knew were important. But he didn't know they were *that* important. He didn't understand that combining these ingredients would create a recipe for a life that was intractable. He didn't know that properly blending these principles would produce a spiritual way of living, which could contagiously, positively, and enduringly benefit others.

Royce's mind continued to wander for several more hours as he quietly lay on the sofa. He was overwhelmed by the lessons he had learned and their potential implications. He thought about the people— like him—who had been living their typical day to day lives and how they also had the rug suddenly pulled out from under them through a variety of circumstances—

death of loved ones, divorce, financial catastrophes, health problems—the list seemed never-ending. Maya was teaching him the magical threads of strength and unlimited power the great masters had woven into their work and their lives, and Royce knew he would have the opportunity—and the obligation—to use it to empower others on their journeys.

At that moment, Royce understood the magnitude of the gift Maya was sharing with him. He said a short, heartfelt prayer of gratitude and fell into a deep sleep.

Royce was awakened the next morning by a knock on his front door. He jumped off the couch as he realized he hadn't budged the entire night. When he reached the door, the delivery person was already scrambling away, but he turned around and offered a smile to Royce and a quick "Have a nice day," then climbed into his truck and headed to his next stop.

As Royce looked down, he saw a small package lying on the doormat in front of him.

He picked it up and reached into his pocket to pull out a penknife and began carefully opening the package. Inside was a book of around 100 pages, entitled *You Will Accomplish Great Things*, with a portrait of a beautiful, refined-looking young Indian woman—likely in her mid-twenties—on the cover. She wore elegant gold bracelets on each wrist, and she was clothed in a traditional, colorful Indian sari. Royce unclipped a short note that was attached to the book and saw it was from Maya. It simply said, "Read this before you visit me today—I will see you after lunch."

Royce thumbed through the book for a few seconds and set it down as he headed in to make his coffee. As it was brewing, he jumped in the shower. He thought about the book, wondering how it could relate to his conversations with Maya or his life in general. There *was* something that looked familiar about the woman on the cover, but after a moment, he dismissed the thought and continued with his shower, still struggling to wake up.

Once he got dressed, Royce headed into the kitchen, grabbed a cup of coffee, and sat down to read the book that had just been delivered.

From the minute he read the first page, he was captivated. It was the story of a young woman who grew up on the streets of Bombay with her three young siblings, her mother, and her grandmother. Despite her seemingly insurmountable challenges, she had risen to become a political leader in her country, and the book was unquestionably one of the most inspirational works he had ever read. In no time, he had devoured the book and felt ready to conquer the world.

Royce gobbled down a quick meal, tidied up a bit, and headed over to Maya's.

When he arrived, he noticed Maya was seated in the gazebo where the little statue was. She appeared to be deep in thought as she gazed at the beautiful piece. When Royce walked up, Maya quickly looked away from the statue and started engaging with him in her usual, cheerful way. Noticing the book in his hands, Maya smiled and said, "I see you got my special delivery."

Royce nodded. "It was special, alright." He sat down beside her and immediately blurted out, "Maya, I have never read anything like that in my life."

She smiled broadly, "I thought you might find it interesting. It ties in well with today's lesson."

"If today's lesson is as inspiring as that book, I'm definitely ready to hear it," Royce said with a smile.

Maya looked at him calmly and said, "Royce, close your eyes. I want you to see something."

A week ago, he would have thought "closing your eyes to see something" was a misspoken, paradoxical phrase. Now, he understood that her words were not misspoken at all.

With Royce's eyes now shut, Maya leaned forward and placed her fingers on his temples as she had done before. Immediately he felt her gentleness and warmth; then, a recognizable scene appeared in his mind. The image was of Royce as a young man in his twenties, standing outside his hotel in Bombay on a sweltering summer morning. He would be in the city for two days before catching a train to Bangalore for the first stop on the Indian professional tennis tour. Royce was about to go to breakfast, but as he stood in the ninety-degree heat, a shoeless young girl about ten years old in a tattered pink dress approached him. It was common, as the streets of Bombay were full of beggars, many of them small children sent by their parents to find unsuspecting foreigners that would "donate" dollars or Indian rupees. Royce smiled at the little girl, and instinctively shook his head as if to say, "I don't have money for you."

It didn't matter. The girl grinned and said to him, in perfect English, "I'm Oocha."

He smiled back and kindly replied, "Very nice to meet you. I'm Royce."

Oocha laughed. "That's a funny name."

Royce raised an eyebrow and chuckled, "Well, I kind of like it—and now I've got to go to breakfast. Nice to meet you, Oocha."

Royce started down the city street, which was crowded with what seemed like thousands of people, along with a huge number of oxen and water buffalo. After a moment, he instinctively turned around, and there was Oocha. He grinned, "I told you, I have no money. I'm a poor tennis player."

Oocha laughed and shrugged her shoulders as Royce turned back around and kept walking toward his breakfast destination. Although he kept his eyes closed, Royce began to come out of his semi-conscious state and wondered why Maya had taken him to this scene in Bombay.

Sensing his impending question, Maya softly said, "There's a reason, Royce. Continue to watch."

Royce nodded and felt himself slipping back into the trancelike world as the vision became clear again. It was the next day, and Royce was again standing in front of his Bombay hotel.

As he stepped onto the sidewalk to go to breakfast, Oocha appeared out of nowhere, grinning.

"Hello, Mr. Royce."

Royce laughed. "You again? I told you, I'm broke."

Instead of a response, Oocha reached up and playfully grabbed his hand and started walking. Royce wondered what the child was up to, but he had a little time to spare, so he let her continue to lead him as she clutched his hand. After a couple of minutes on the streets, Oocha approached the side of an old building where there was a metal staircase with a sheet pulled across the opening below the first flight of stairs. Oocha gently let Royce's hand go and then carefully pulled back the sheet.

He wasn't prepared for what he saw.

It was a woman who was likely Oocha's mother, her grandmother, and three small children, all living in a makeshift room under the stairs. Royce tried to hide his shock, but when he looked at Oocha, tears rolled down his cheek.

Oocha smiled and said, "My family." Despite her horribly adverse urban circumstances, she was *proud* for Royce to meet her clan.

Royce sat on the filthy ground and tried to speak with the family members, which was nearly impossible, except for Oocha translating some of his words into Hindi. After a few moments, he gracefully said goodbye, stood, and stepped outside of the makeshift house with Oocha. Royce, knowing today would be the last day he would ever see the little girl, was filled with compassion. He picked her up gently, looked tenderly at her and said, "Oocha, you are a very smart, wonderful girl. Someday you will accomplish great things." As if to make sure there was no mistake in what she heard, he repeated, "You will accomplish great things."

With those words, Royce reached in his pocket and pulled out twenty dollars—his allotted meal money for the day—and handed it to Oocha, which she accepted as if she had just won the Indian lottery. The little girl turned and again raised the sheet over the staircase and disappeared to hand the money to her mother.

As Royce walked away toward the next street corner, he turned back to see a smiling Oocha, waving and yelling without concern as to who heard. "Mr. Royce, I will accomplish great things!"

Royce nodded and smiled, waved to her one last time, and then rounded the corner, out of Oocha's sight.

Deeply perplexed, Royce opened his eyes. "Maya, my words to her—the words she echoed to me when I last saw her on that street—they were the same as the title of the book you had me read today. I don't understand. How . . ."

Maya looked kindly into his eyes and softly interrupted him. "Royce, you did not see the dedication of the book. Let me show you." She opened the book and read the words aloud. "To Royce, whose compassionate and powerful words changed me forever—and may my words do the same for each person who reads this book." The dedication concluded with the author's name, Indra Anand.

"You don't mean that Indra Anand is . . . *Oocha*?" Royce said in an incredulous tone.

Maya slowly nodded. "She wrote under a pen name because she feared retaliation by the authorities for her inspirational work to rally young Indian women to become successful in business and life. It was definitely a man's world at that time in India, and her writing and speaking were, well, let's just say, not as popular among the male-dominated government."

She continued. "Royce, I met Oocha several years after you met her. I was visiting schools as part of a peace project in Bombay, and this young girl stood out from the crowd. Regardless of the label that had been put on her due to her lower caste, when I spoke with her, I knew she was special. I decided to provide the funds to make a university education possible for her once she finished high school. After she graduated from university, she became an esteemed leader in the Indian women's rights movement, especially with younger women.

"But she would tell you today, as she told me, that none of what she has done would be possible if she had not met you when she was a child."

Royce was flabbergasted. "What a small, small world—such a coincidence," he gasped.

Maya nodded. "I agree it is a small world. However, I believe there are no coincidences. Everyone and everything is presented to us as our teacher to guide us, instruct us, and remind us that we are all connected in so many ways. Some ways are obvious, some are invisible, but we are all related, and the ripple effects of what we do may be felt locally and quickly, or across the world, years later—as in this case."

Royce nodded in agreement, still recovering from Maya's revelation about Oocha.

"But Royce," she continued, "this incident is also a perfect example of the fifth principle, and that is this. . .

THE PRINCIPLE OF INSPIRATIONAL WORDS

"One of the things that became clear to Mr. Gandhi as he studied the texts was the power that all the words seemed to convey. Regardless of which language, which part of the world, which religion, the words had a connotation of strength, goodness, and hope. The words were always carefully chosen, and they were ones that would impact the reader in a way that was unquestionably constructive. Even though their teachings were educating and enlightening, the writers never came across as mandating or fear-evoking."

Royce leaned in attentively.

"Words are powerful tools. Whether they are written or spoken, they contain spiritual elements that can be influential in many ways and on many levels, yet the importance of inspirational language is often overlooked. Many times, people want to grow spiritually, and so they study and exercise great self-discipline, but then they use words in ways that are incompatible with how they are otherwise living or with the type of people they want to become. It essentially negates what they are trying to accomplish."

Royce nodded his understanding and agreement as Maya continued.

"Self-limiting and pessimistic-oriented words like can't, don't, won't, never, shouldn't, wouldn't, all have a basis in lack and doubt. So, not only do these types of words weaken us, the weakness is contagiously disempowering to those who come in contact with us."

Royce chimed in, "I know exactly what you mean. When I am writing my books, I feel strong and encouraged. Based on what you are saying, it's likely because I am focused on using words that will empower and encourage my readers. The words benefit the reader—and the writer."

"Indeed, Royce," added Maya. "The spiritual greats were so habitual in using inspirational, optimistic language that there was little difference between the speaker and the speech. The encouraging words had simply become a part of them, like a hand or foot. But I will caution you; it takes great practice to reach that level of conditioned behavior. For example, you will seldom hear me use the word 'no' or its derivatives. Of course, there are exceptions. For instance, if I am seeing or experiencing something fundamentally wrong which needs to be addressed, I may choose those types of words. However, typically by using less conflict-oriented words, I can get my point across effectively and thereby avoid a potentially unpleasant or resistant reaction."

"Give me an example, please," Royce said.

Maya proceeded. "In a conversation, if I disagree with you and tell you 'no, you are wrong,' you will likely become defensive. However, if I carefully listen to you and then want to disagree, I will find something within your statement or context to agree with—which you could call aligning—then I will share a different way of looking at it, which is called shifting. By authentically honoring something in your statement, I honor you, and you will be much more likely to listen to my counterpoint. The word 'no' or any form of that subtly discredits what you are saying—and it may seem that I am discrediting *you*."

"Isn't that manipulation?" Royce asked.

"I call it tact, deference, and effective nonresistance," Maya answered.

Royce laughed. "OK, I guess you're right. I *have* noticed that you seldom correct me or tell me I am wrong during our conversations. I thought it was because I was *right* every time," he grinned. "Now I see when you disagreed, you have expressed that disagreement by supporting me, yet redirecting my comments."

"Yes, that's true." She smiled. "Now let me give you another example of using inspirational language. Many people commonly use other words that are inadvertently disempowering and victimizing." Royce looked surprised as Maya continued. "They use phrases like "have to" or "got to" or "need to." Although these seem to be innocuous phrases, they are self-limiting. They are essentially confirming the person has no choice in whatever they are referring to doing. There are underlying pessimistic qualities inherent in those phrases which tend to sink into the subconscious mind and reinforce a stress-inducing mentality of having no option."

"Incredible," Royce said. "I'm sure I use those words sometimes, if not often. I just didn't realize those types of phrases were negative."

"The vast majority of people don't realize they are doing the same thing, often all day long. The *Six Principles of Sacred Power* clearly points out the consistent use of optimistic, non-victimizing words that each of the spiritual masters used in their writings. It's almost as if these wise men collaborated on the fact that the words we use are not simply words; they are the foundation of our lives."

Royce continued to listen carefully, as Maya concluded. "I could say that the two examples I just shared are small examples of inspirational language instruction, which in one way they are. In another way, they are the *main* points—the roots of the whole fifth principle. Inspirational verbiage and intonation are based on possibility, encouragement, love, and faith. Those traits have divine power, and they have the potential to change lives in a great way. Pessimistic, mandating, judgmental, discouragement-oriented words and phrases do the opposite—and have equal potential—in a destructive way both for the speaker and the listener."

"Or the writer and the reader," affirmed Royce. "I have shared with my readers that their words create or destroy the world—their world and the world of others."

"True," Maya said. "Words properly used, like your words to Oocha, can begin or encourage someone to continue on a journey to greatness. As you have seen by that outcome, words can inspire someone to do what may typically be thought of as impossible. A spiritually mature person understands this awesome power and therefore wisely chooses their words."

Royce sat quietly, absorbing Maya's summation.

After several seconds of peaceful silence, Maya looked at him and calmly concluded. "That is all for today, Royce. Tomorrow we will discuss the sixth and final principle. The day will be exceptionally powerful, and I know you are ready."

Royce nodded in agreement. Oddly enough, he was starting to feel ready for *anything*—or so he thought.

CHAPTER 10

Royce awoke the next morning mentally and physically refreshed and prepared for the day. He thought about how far his life had come since meeting Maya. The pain he had felt prior to that time was still there, of course, but there was a feeling of strength that overshadowed the pain. Although he knew the times ahead would be challenging, he now had a renewed sense of purpose and courage. He quickly showered, grabbed his coffee and a bagel, and headed out the door for his upcoming lesson.

When he arrived, Maya stepped out to greet him and saw the coffee cup held gently in his right hand. "Shall I pour you a fresh cup before we start?" she asked.

"I think you know my caffeine needs pretty well at this point." He laughed. "Yes, that would be great."

When Maya went inside, Royce sat in a chair on the porch and saw the copy of *The Six Principles of Sacred Power* lying on a small table. His mind wandered back to the previous week before he knew anything of the book. Royce thought about how he felt then—distraught, exhausted, hopeless. Now, his life had been transformed, and he fully understood the powerful capabilities of the manuscript.

When Maya returned, she said, "Why don't we stay on the porch today, Royce? The day is sunny, and the view from here is still one of my favorites."

"Works for me, Coach," Royce cheerfully replied.

Maya laughed. "I've never been called Coach before I met you, and I kind of like it. Today's principle relates to a concept that every good coach understands, but likely not at the level we are going to discuss."

As a former athlete, Royce's ears perked up.

Maya continued, "The sixth principle is this . . .

THE PRINCIPLE OF
UNRELENTING PERSISTENCE

"Mr. Gandhi saved this principle for last, although it is of paramount significance. He knew that even if one had every other principle in place in their lives, if the element of persistence was not added, the spiritual seeker would eventually falter and then fail in their quest.

"The masters understood this concept all too well. Each of them were persecuted for their ways, beliefs, and teachings, and at times they felt like giving up, just like any of us do. However, they had such certainty in the importance of their work; they refused to quit.

Royce reflected and said, "I remember seeing the best tennis players in the world on the tour. When they competed, they would never, ever give up, no matter how tired, discouraged, or uncomfortable they were—they just kept going. I met a young player in Brazil who had been on the tour for eight years and he had been to fifty-three countries, but had never broken into the world rankings. He told me he would not stop until he made it. His money had run out when he was in Spain, midway through his second year. But after he lost out of the competition there, he found a low-paying service job, which he worked at until he saved enough to go back to the tournament life. Every time he ran out of funds, no matter what country he was in, he would somehow find a job to pay for his basic needs. He would practice all day and work all night—he was driven.

"Someone told me that at the end of his eighth year of trying, in Malaysia, he won a tournament that pushed him into the world rankings; he had reached his goal through incredible persistence."

Maya nodded. "He would never quit. That's a great illustration of the type of persistence Mr. Gandhi found woven through the sacred doctrines. It's a rare trait, but it is critical for the kind of work you and I are doing. The person who is not indoctrinated with this understanding would think extra effort is all there is to persistence. Extra effort is simply the *beginning*. Unrelenting persistence requires patience beyond what many would think to be humanly possible—but it *is* possible. When we develop this mentality that nothing can stop us, there is virtually nothing that *can* stop us. Criticism cannot. Competition cannot. Adverse conditions cannot. Every obstacle we face with a patient, ultra-persistent mindset simply becomes the next thing that is put in front of us on our journey. Once we begin, the rest is simply a matter of tenaciously pressing on."

She continued. "Lao Tzu used the metaphor of water when he talked about this concept of utmost patience and persistence. He referenced water, as soft as it is, as having the ability to eventually overcome every hard thing that opposes it. It's an excellent example of what we are capable of when we develop these traits. It's not about physical strength; it's about having an unfaltering will."

Royce was inspired, but then again, he had been inspired every day since he met Maya. He was feeling increasingly as if he was becoming the person she had said he was capable of becoming through the absorption of the Six Principles. Even as an inspirational author, *this* was a realm he wasn't familiar with. The combination of traits he had learned was exhilarating . . . freeing. Yet he also had a distinct understanding that all he had learned was not just to benefit *him*. It was for the betterment of humankind. *Could that be possible? Is it arrogant to think I can be an instrument to make an impact on the world like this?*

Maya interrupted his thoughts. "Royce, I know what you are thinking. Yes, it is possible."

Royce laughed. "Do you always know my thoughts?"

Maya smiled and replied, "No, thankfully. I have enough going through my own head. So, your secrets are safe." She smiled even more broadly and added, "Well, most of them."

Royce grinned and playfully rolled his eyes.

"Back to the lesson at hand, my good man," Maya said.

"Ah yes, persistence. Unrelenting persistence," he said.

Maya moved on quickly. "Every historical figure Mr. Gandhi studied was immersed in the type of persistence we are talking about. Most people don't fully understand that these spiritual leaders went through incredibly challenging times—*extraordinarily* challenging times. People typically hear what they want to hear, and they see what they want to see. They don't want to believe that there was a huge price for these teachers to pay along the way, because that would mean they would have to go through some of the same challenges. It's much easier to fantasize that successful people are simply overnight successes. But it's not reality. The spiritual giants knew this, and so they developed and eventually embodied this dogged perseverance and presented it in their writings."

Maya looked at her watch and realized it was already one o'clock. "Royce, I've fixed us a little picnic today. Why don't you go sit by the creek near the back garden? You'll see a small table and two chairs. I will get our lunch and meet you in a few moments."

Royce nodded and walked around to the back, where a well-worn path led to the place by the stream where Maya would join him.

Royce reached his destination and sat in the chair and gazed at his surroundings. He had been so engrossed in Maya's instruction over the past week that he had begun taking the beauty of the property for granted. He thought back to the first day he met Maya and how the gardens mesmerized him. Ironic, he thought, even with the stunning beauty all around him for the last week, it was Maya and her teachings that mesmerized him.

Hearing footsteps behind him, Royce turned to see Maya walking toward him with their lunch in a small wicker basket. He tried not to stare, but the sun shining from behind through her long black hair gave her an almost angelic presence. She smiled at Royce and asked, "Hungry?"

"Absolutely," he quickly replied.

Maya placed the basket by the table and removed its contents—a delectable-looking combination of fresh vegetables, hummus, and some freshly baked Indian bread. "I hope you like naan," Maya grinned.

"Actually, I do," Royce countered. "I learned to love it when I was in India, and I'm addicted."

The two of them chatted non-stop as they ate until their meal was finished. It seemed they never ran out of subjects to talk about. At one point, Royce asked, "Maya, what happened to all of the other leaders in the freedom movement—the ones who received copies of the book from Mr. Gandhi?"

Maya's words had a tone of nostalgia as she replied. "After my father fled India with me and my mom, each of them did the same with their families. They ended up in a variety of countries—Nepal, Tibet, even Cambodia."

Royce nodded. "Understandable. These are all predominantly Hindu countries." Then he grinned and added, "And I also can't help but notice that those countries were all distinctly *not* British colonies."

Maya smiled. "You are correct, Royce, that was no coincidence." She continued, "But now, each of the original owners of the books has passed away, and the manuscripts have been handed down to the recipients of their choice. Three chose family members, and two others chose persons that were very close to them."

"Do you stay in contact with them?" Royce wondered aloud.

"Yes," Maya said. "We get together at least once per year, and as you can imagine, our bond is extremely strong due to the unique common denominator our relationships have."

Royce nodded his understanding.

The rest of the afternoon flew by as the conversation flowed easily, and the two never left their spot by the creek. As the early evening approached, Maya seemed to grow increasingly reflective, and then at one point, she gently said, "Royce, you now know all of the lessons from the *Six Principles of Sacred Power.*"

As if he knew what Maya was about to say next, Royce interjected, "Maya, there must be so much more for me to learn. . ."

Maya broke in. "Yes, there always will be more to learn, but now you are a changed person, as I was changed by the principles of the book. Now it's time for you to share the fruits of your labor. The world needed your gift before you met me, but now the gift you have will benefit the world at a whole new level."

Royce persisted. "Maya, you can do things that I cannot do, and you can do things I don't believe I will *ever* be able to do . . ."

Maya stopped him, saying, "Royce, I have shared things with you in ways which were designed not to show you what *I* could do, but to show you what *you* would be able to do. Many of these acts are what you might call miraculous, and maybe that is what they are. But a miraculous event is often relative. For example, if someone one hundred years ago saw an airplane take off, they would say it was miraculous; today, it is simply commonplace. Likewise, one hundred years before that, if someone saw a light bulb turn on, they would assume that would be something only available to magicians or wizards. Now, electricity is a part of our daily routine. There are thousands of examples."

Royce was starting to understand her perspective, but Maya continued before he could speak. "If a ninety-pound woman lifts a car off of a person that she sees is trapped under it, would that not be a miracle? Even feats which superior athletes have accomplished would surely be thought of as impossible at some previous time. That is what I mean by the *relative nature of miracles*. Royce, tell me, do you understand?"

Royce paused for several seconds, then nodded and replied quietly but confidently. "Maya, when I first met you, I knew that you were special. With your incredible skills in the garden, your ability to understand human nature, and the powerful spiritual concepts you've taught me, you are a constant inspiration. I have learned principles which have already affected my life in ways I could never have dreamed of, and now I know it is my obligation—no, my humble yet great opportunity— to use these sacred principles to carry out the mission that the great spiritual leaders taught. That mission, which you have shown me, is to help others realize the God-given power they have to change themselves and the world. Understanding the Six Principles has been like scales falling from my eyes. I see the world in a new way that is full of more hope, love, and unlimited opportunities. But as these principles become more ingrained in my life, I must recognize and *believe* in the extraordinary potential for greatness that I have so I can teach others to have the same belief. Never again will I speak in terms of doubt, as I know that my belief is the foundation of my potential greatness, and with that trust, all things are possible. Without it, virtually *nothing* worthwhile is possible."

Maya sat quietly, and then a slight smile appeared as she said, "Royce, you have learned the lessons as I had no doubt you would, and I am sure you will use this knowledge to heal and empower people, who will, in turn, heal and empower others. It's now time for the student to become not just the teacher, but the teacher of teachers, and our world will be a much better place because of that."

She became silent again, and in an unusually contemplative way, added, "Royce, come back tomorrow. I have one more thing to share with you."

Royce felt a sinking feeling in the pit of his stomach. Throughout these days with Maya, his intuition had been steadily increasing to where it was now at a level that even *he* could not comprehend. But what he *could* comprehend was that his intuition was telling him the lessons were about to take a different turn . . . and he wasn't sure he liked it.

CHAPTER 11

Unlike most of the previous six nights, Royce tossed and turned. There was so much going through his mind—so many questions. But the most prevalent question was, *what is Maya going to tell me?* As they had parted, her look and demeanor seemed distinctively different—even troubled. Was something wrong? Did she need his help? Was there some clue or comment he had missed? He didn't know, but he would soon find out because after a restless night of thinking, it was daylight. Royce dragged himself out of bed and into his morning routine.

After a shower and breakfast, he grabbed a coffee for the road and headed toward Maya's. Unlike the past few sunny and hot days, there was a heavy cloud covering, a light sprinkle, and slightly cooler temperatures, which greeted Royce as he began his journey. He reflected on the lessons he had learned, and as he cruised down the road—even in his state of fatigue—Royce realized how relaxed he was. He was breathing slowly and deeply. He held the steering wheel gently instead of gripping it tightly like he often found himself doing in previous months. As he continued down the road, he found himself uttering words of appreciation for various, seemingly random sights along the way—the green pasture, the red dirt side roads, the birds flying so freely through the Georgia sky. He even gave thanks for the weather, although the rain was coming down at a steady pace as he pulled into Maya's driveway.

After parking his car, Royce walked up the path to Maya's house. What he then saw stopped him in his tracks. Maya was sitting on the porch in a pink raincoat, and beside her were two suitcases. His intuition had, unfortunately, been right. Royce felt the blood drain out of his face as he began walking slowly toward her.

"Namaste," Maya softly said as Royce ambled up the stairs and weakly poured himself into the chair beside her.

"Namaste," he said, managing to smile. He then sarcastically added, "With my newfound wisdom, I get the idea that you may be leaving."

Maya smiled compassionately and said, "Royce, I know this is a surprise to you, and in some ways, it is a surprise to me."

Royce raised his eyebrows and asked, "What do you mean in some ways?"

Maya edged closer, then reached over and gently clasped Royce's hands. The tender look in her beautiful brown eyes added to the melancholy as she began slowly speaking. "Royce, do you remember on our second day in the garden, I told you that I would likely be returning to India soon?"

Royce nodded tentatively.

"I didn't know when or why, but as I have told you, I seldom question events in my life anymore," she affirmed.

Royce interrupted in a whisper, "Part of a bigger plan, right?"

Maya smiled and replied, "Yes." She continued. "Two days ago, when I shared with you that I had pressing matters, I had just received news from a trusted friend in India that Rajiv was only days from passing away. He had apparently been ill for many months."

Royce was shocked. "Rajiv? Your former bodyguard . . . and fiancé'?"

"Correct. My friend thought I would like to know, even though I had not seen Rajiv since well before I left India," Maya said.

Royce was still trying to make sense of it all as he asked, "But . . . why are you leaving, Maya? You even said that you don't look back because it's not the direction you're planning on going. Your life is here now, right?"

Maya paused and then continued. "My direction and my plans must stay fluid, Royce. And remember, for each of us, our home and our life are wherever we choose to make them. Now, it appears mine will need to be India, at least for a while."

"I still don't understand," Royce stammered.

Maya took a deep breath and then added, "Early this morning, I received news that Rajiv had died. The caller, an advisor of Rajiv's, also had more to tell me."

Royce's puzzled look urged her forward with her story.

"Apparently, after the last time I saw Rajiv, he began working in law enforcement just outside of New Delhi. He continued to move up in rank and years later was elected to a political office. He developed quite a following due to his platform of political reform, and soon, he was elected to a position of high rank in the Bharatiya Janata Party, which is the more conservative wing in India. When he died, he had amassed a substantial fortune from a tea plantation he owned."

Royce pondered aloud, "But, how does this affect you, Maya?"

She sat quietly and then slowly answered. "According to the advisor, when Rajiv passed, he left everything to me. The business, his home—everything. He never married, and in his will, he stated that I was the only one he ever loved and the only one he would ever love."

Tears trickled down Maya's cheeks as she continued. "Rajiv also asked if I would assume his political position in the Union Territory of Delhi. I received another message this morning from an Indian government official in which he confirmed Rajiv's request and added that within the Indian Constitution, this type of transfer of power is legal. It is potentially subject to congressional ratification, but since my father had a history with Mr. Gandhi and the people of the Union Territory of Delhi, as did I, it should be easily endorsed."

Royce gulped. "This is incredible, Maya."

Maya nodded. "I am still in shock. Royce, due to the work Rajiv did decreasing political corruption, I believe the climate in government has greatly changed from the old guard I was fighting against years ago. With Rajiv's passing, I feel led to return and continue the work of answering the unified cries of the people for civil rights and ethical change."

"You'll need help. How will you find a team?" Royce asked.

Maya smiled. "I trust the process will unfold exactly as it should, Royce. I have already been in touch with an old acquaintance of yours who has agreed to be my right-hand person, much like my father was to Mr. Gandhi."

Royce looked puzzled. "Who?"

Maya looked into Royce's eyes with reassurance as she calmly said, "Oocha, Royce. She is now one of the most influential women in all of India. To have her by my side will be nothing short of magnificent as we seek to shape the direction of the country."

Tears welled up in Royce's eyes as he noticed Maya's look of intensity and passion. He knew it was time. "You have no choice, Maya. The people need you, and you need them. I vouch for the fact that you and the special gifts you bring will transform lives and the country, just as I have been transformed. The winds of change are blowing."

As if on cue, a strong breeze blew across the porch as Maya looked deeply into Royce's eyes. His heart was beating like it would explode as Maya leaned forward and tenderly kissed him. It seemed their entire lifetimes—so different, yet in some ways so alike—were colliding in one lingering, spiritual moment.

Though their embrace only lasted seconds, it felt like hours—wonderful, magical hours.

As Royce gently pulled away and began to open his eyes, his thoughts were everywhere. *What will I say next? What will she say next? Where will this lead—if anywhere at all?* As he opened his eyes, Royce's wonderings were stopped cold.

Maya was . . . gone.

"This can't be," he said to himself incredulously. But it was. Her suitcases had also vanished. Royce sprang to his feet and dashed toward the front door and flung it open. His heart sank as he saw every object in Maya's home had disappeared, except for a table with two items resting on it. He moved closer and recognized both of them instantly. The first was a copy of *The*

Six Principles of Sacred Power—it was Maya's copy; he knew without question. Royce took a deep breath as he reached over to pick up the second item—the small bronze statue which he had admired so many times in the garden gazebo. Trembling and fighting back tears, Royce put the statue down and picked up the manuscript. Protruding from the book was the edge of a small envelope with his name on it, which he eagerly but carefully opened. Reading the words felt surreal.

Royce,

> *In one of our early conversations, I remember sharing with you that I did not know what brought us together, and that was true. So many times in my life, I wondered where I was being led and why I was being led there, only to find out each time that I was exactly where I needed to be.*

> *Now once again, I have found this trust to be affirmed.*

> *I see clearly that the reason our lives have intersected was to help heal you, to help heal me, and now, for you especially, to use your gifts to heal the world.*

> *My copy of The Six Principles of Sacred Power you see here is now yours. It symbolizes and avows the power you have discovered. Live out its lessons, and know you are free to pass it and its message along as I did—and like me, you will know when the time is right.*

What you have learned so well is that we all have abilities that would appear to be miraculous, yet those abilities are hidden underneath stratums of fears, anxieties, and doubts. Only when we find and remove those hindrances, can we expose the magnificent tools that have always been accessible to each of us. Sadly, most people do not realize what they have available to them, but with the sacred principles you have come to know, hopefully, you can change this. I believe you can . . . and will.

The statue, I am so honored to share with you. It was first given to my parents by Mr. Gandhi, who had commissioned its creation by a magnificent sculptor in Madras. The piece represented my parents' work together in the movement. The star, of course, is India, and they are looking to it as they dream of a bright future for all citizens. Each time you look at it, let the figures and their upward, unified gaze remind you of the common work we are doing— although from different sides of the world.

You are a new man now, Royce. You understand that the ability to perform what some would call miracles is only limited by one's own belief. Your daughters, your friends, and other people in your life, will sense the spirit of unlimited belief you now have, and it will bless them.

You have your work to do, and I have mine, but someday I know our paths will cross again. Until then, I wish you Godspeed and great things on your journey ahead.

Namaste,

Maya

Royce slowly, numbly took one final look around the house, gathered his two precious keepsakes, and walked out to his car for the trip home.

Driving away from the cottage and the immaculate gardens, Royce noticed the rain had stopped, and the clouds were starting to clear away. Surprisingly, although he felt the pain of knowing his time with Maya was over, he also felt *happy*. The thought occurred to him that he had been honored beyond imagination to have spent this time with her and to be privy to *The Six Principles of Sacred Power*. A feeling of exhilaration began spreading over him as he thought of the possibilities—a feeling he knew would make Maya proud.

Maybe she was right—maybe he was a new man.

As the car gained momentum, Royce glanced down at the cup holder in the console beside him and noticed the half-finished cup of coffee, which had gotten cold. *What a pity*, he thought. It was the perfect time to have a nice warm cup of java to celebrate Maya as he headed away from her home for the last time. Putting his eyes back on the winding road, he instinctively felt for the cup and then gently clasped it as he became lost in thought.

Suddenly, Royce became acutely aware of the cup's increasing warmth and the steam lazily rising from its dark brown contents.

He smiled broadly and lifted the cup to his lips. Yes, Royce Holloway was indeed. . . a brand-new man.

The inspiration continues in The Mystic's Gift/Royce Holloway series with book 2, *The Gentleman's Journey*.

THE SIX PRINCIPLES OF SACRED POWER

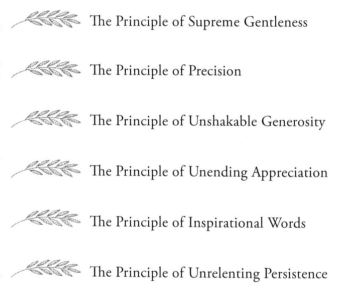

The Principle of Supreme Gentleness

The Principle of Precision

The Principle of Unshakable Generosity

The Principle of Unending Appreciation

The Principle of Inspirational Words

The Principle of Unrelenting Persistence

AUTHOR'S NOTES

I'm not sure about other authors, but each time I write a book, something happens behind the scenes in my life to make the book unique.

The Mystic's Gift was no exception. Here's why. . .

This book was based on a short story I wrote entitled *Life Lessons from a Master Gardener*, which turned out to be very popular among my readers. However, even though I had a clear picture of the "mystic" type of person the main character (later to be known as Maya) was, I never identified her nationality in the short story because I had never determined it.

As I began writing *The Mystic's Gift*, I knew I needed to give the character a nationality. But which country would she be from? For a variety of reasons, I narrowed it down to Spain, Australia, Italy, and India.

After weeks of wrestling with this question, I decided that India was my choice. I would have one of her parents be from London, England, and one from India—and center the plot around experiences that occurred during the time of the British occupation of India.

Although I felt fairly certain this was the right nationality direction; I wasn't one hundred percent sure.

Until this happened . . .

The night before I was to begin writing the book, my wife and I decided to try a new restaurant near our home. It was a drizzly Georgia evening, but we chose to sit in a covered outdoor section of the restaurant to enjoy the warm summer air.

As we sat at the table and began sipping our wine, a woman in her early seventies seated one table over began speaking to us.

She was very kind, interesting, and it turns out, she was well-traveled. She had a slight accent, and after a few moments of our conversation with this fascinating woman, I asked her about her accent (I incorrectly guessed it was Scottish).

Her answer? "It's English. I'm half British and half Indian. My dad was from India, and my mother was from London."

My jaw dropped.

Not only had she just "coincidentally" validated my character's heritage, but she was the first person I *ever* recall meeting who was half British and half Indian.

So, Indra, wherever you are, thank you. From the time of that affirmation until the time I finished this book, *The Mystic's Gift* was a journey of pure joy.

Skip

ACKNOWLEDGMENTS

I am grateful to have had such a wonderful, gifted team to help me with this book.

My editor and proofreader Terry Stafford, my cover designer and interior formatter, Dino Marino, and members of my Advance Reader Team—all have helped bring this book to life.

I also want to express gratitude to my wife, Anne Marie, who encouraged me to write my first fiction book.

Finally, I would like to thank my friends Dwight Crum, Ken Guy, and Kathy Lubbers. Their comments helped steer the direction of the book in just the right way at just the needed time.

ABOUT
SKIP JOHNSON

Skip Johnson is an award-winning inspirational author whose goal is to empower, inspire, and enrich the lives of his readers.

He is known for his easy-going style of adventurous storytelling, with rich elements of spirituality, mysticism, and personal growth woven throughout his books. One prominent aspect of Skip's writing is how he takes readers on symbolic journeys of self-discovery and enlightenment. His characters often find themselves on treks to faraway places where meetings with wise mystical mentors lead readers to contemplate their own personal and spiritual journeys and how their lives can be more fulfilling and joyful.

His storytelling is simple yet profound, allowing readers from all walks of life to extract and quickly apply the nuggets of wisdom, compassion, and peacefulness that permeate the pages of his narratives. He uses crystal-clear imagery to create the feeling for readers of being right beside each character on their life-changing, heroic journey in every saga.

Skip's books are both spiritual and practical. Each story encourages readers to look inside themselves for the magic, courage, and strength that is often deeply hidden within themselves, patiently waiting to be released to powerfully impact the world.

Based in Georgia, Skip himself has traveled many paths, including that of a motivational speaker, a business leader, a master tennis professional, and a world traveler. These experiences have shaped his writing, and the wisdom and insights woven into each story leave readers filled with wonder, gratitude, and enthusiasm for the days ahead.

His works have earned various award designations, including the Maxy Awards Book of the Year, the International Book Award, and the Nautilus Silver Winner Award.

To see all of Skip's books and free e-books, visit https://www.skipjohnsonauthor.com/.

CAN I ASK A FAVOR?

First of all, thank you for reading my book! Would you do me a favor and take a moment to write a short review on Amazon? Reviews are so important to authors like me, and if you would share your thoughts so others can find out about my writing, I would be truly grateful. If you do write a review, feel free to let me know by dropping me an email at skipjohnsonauthor1@gmail.com so I can personally tell you thanks!